For Janice and Laura

DOING TEAM ETHNOGRAPHY
Warnings and Advice

KEN C. ERICKSON
University of Missouri-Kansas City

DONALD D. STULL
University of Kansas

Qualitative Research Methods Series
Volume 42

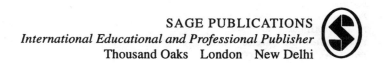

SAGE PUBLICATIONS
International Educational and Professional Publisher
Thousand Oaks   London   New Delhi

For information:

 SAGE Publications, Inc.
2455 Teller Road
Thousand Oaks, California 91320
E-mail: order@sagepub.com

SAGE Publications Ltd.
6 Bonhill Street
London EC2A 4PU
United Kingdom

SAGE Publications India Pvt. Ltd.
M-32 Market
Greater Kailash I
New Delhi 110 048 India

Printed in the United States of America

Library of Congress Cataloging-in-Publication Data

Erickson, Ken C.
   Doing team ethnography: warnings and advice/by Ken C. Erickson
and Donald D. Stull
     p. cm.—(Qualitative research methods; v. 42)
   Includes bibliographical references.
   ISBN 0-7619-0666-5 (acid-free paper).—ISBN 0-7619-0667-3
(pbk.: acid-free paper)
   1. Ethnology—Methodology. 2. Ethnology—Research. 3. Ethnology—
field work. 4. Research teams. I. Stull, Donald D. II. Title. III. Series.
GN33.E73 1997   97-4911
305.8′007′23—dc21

98 99 00 01 02 03 10 9 8 7 6 5 4 3 2 1

Acquiring Editor:	Peter Labella
Editorial Assistant:	Corinne Pierce
Production Editor:	Sherrise M. Purdum
Production Assistant:	Karen Wiley
Typesetter/Designer:	Marion Warren
Print Buyer:	Anna Chin

CONTENTS

The question of how ethnographers bring forth believable, credible results from their studies that command reader respect is one on which much ink is spilled with no end in sight. Method primers abound, confessional tales multiply, and increasingly adroit epistemological rationales for (and against) ethnographies are put forward. Attention moves from researched to researcher, from theory to data, from ideal to practice, from writer to reader (and back again). Fieldwork, once understood as a relatively simple if lengthy process of building rapport with members of a studied community—an achieved friendship built on mutual understanding and empathetic concern—is now presented as something closer to a complex, difficult process of alliance-building involving various forms of disclosure, dispute, negotiation, coercion, complicity, respect, companionship, ironic toleration, collaboration, and advocacy.

Yet, in the midst of seasonal crises and waves of repositioning and reconceptualizing ethnography, one element has remained much the same. It has remained so since Malinowski turned away from calling native informants up to the verandah for a highly scripted chat and pushed back the flap of his tent to sally forth on his own and "do the village." With few exceptions, ethnography is portrayed—both descriptively and prescriptively—as an individual undertaking best summarized perhaps by the politically incorrect and historically inaccurate *bon mot* "one man, one tribe."

The *bon mot* is also something of a legacy that passes from generation to generation of anthropologically-oriented fieldworkers and it is one that shapes what Ken Erickson and Don Stull call, with conspiratorial glee, the Lone Ranger approach to ethnography. This is a model with considerable staying power but one they take to task in *Doing Team Ethnography,* the 42nd volume of the Sage series on **Qualitative Research Methods.** Beginning with a backward glance at late 19th-century fieldwork—both the British form of "expedition ethnography" and the American style of "reservation ethnography"—the authors show that collective research projects have played a major role—perhaps even a founding role—in the art and science of the fieldwork trade. Team ethnography has been with us for a very long time and, as demonstrated, for some very good if often ignored reasons.

These methodological matters are neatly laid out by Erickson and Stull who draw on several of their own well-regarded studies for illustrations of the virtues and vices, pleasures and agonies of team ethnography. The work is organized sequentially as a field work guide—from inception to completion, entry to exit, conception to publication. Each section is written with a sense of experience put forth in a deliberately chosen crisp and practical language. The result is a tasty mix of history, story, illustration, advise and wit. The team approach advocated in the monograph is not put forward as some kind of industrial strength ethnography emphasizing collective discipline or obedience to rules and authority. To the contrary, the spirit of team ethnography evoked by the authors is emergent, communal and craftlike, defined only as it is being done in a highly interactive and always tentative fashion. Under the conditions set out by Erickson and Stull, team ethnography is indeed an attractive alternative to the Lone Ranger approach and one surely worth our highest form of praise: imitation.

—John Van Maanen
Peter K. Manning
Marc L. Miller

ACKNOWLEDGMENTS

We are grateful to Louise Lamphere, who recommended us to John Van Maanen for this book. We are especially grateful to him for patiently waiting the 4 years it took us to get up the nerve to write it, for giving us enough rope and the time to get tangled in it, for making his suggestions on early drafts, and, most of all, for putting up with a couple of "cowboy junkies." Happy Boxing Day, John.

Louise Lamphere, Lou Heib, and Kristen Esterberg made helpful suggestions on various chapters. We appreciate their insights and willingness to offer them.

This book is not about the Changing Relations Project or about Garden City, Kansas, but it could not have been written without both of them. For the rest of the Ford Gang—Michael Broadway, Janet Benson, Art Campa, Jose Cintron, and Mark Grey—we enjoyed riding with you. For the people of Garden City, so many of whom have become our friends, colleagues, and collaborators in research and practice, thanks for letting us take our dallies in your corral.

And to Frank Hamilton Cushing and so many other ethnographers who came after—the lone rangers, the annie oakleys, and the sonsofpioneers alike—thanks for blazing the trail.

DOING TEAM ETHNOGRAPHY
Warnings and Advice*

KEN C. ERICKSON
University of Missouri-Kansas City

DONALD D. STULL
University of Kansas

1. AND A RIVER WENT OUT OF EDEN[1]

It was not until I was alone in the district that I began to make some headway; and, at any rate, I found out where lay the secret of effective fieldwork. . . . The principles of method can be grouped under three main headings; first of all, naturally, the student must possess real scientific aims, and know the values and criteria of modern ethnography. Secondly, he ought to put himself in good conditions of work. That is, in the main, to live without other white men, right among the natives. *Finally, he has to apply a number of special methods of collecting, manipulating and fixing his evidence.*

—Bronislaw Malinowski (1922/ 1984, p. 6, emphasis added)

1

---

*With apologies to Rosalie Wax.

In a tent on a South Sea island, Bronislaw Malinowski discovered how to "evoke the real spirit of the natives, the true picture of tribal life," and his introduction to *Argonauts of the Western Pacific* became "the book of Genesis in the fieldworker's bible" (Van Maanen, 1988, p. 10; see also Malinowski, 1922/1984). We have canonized Malinowski for creating modern fieldwork "in May 1915 . . . when he set up his tent in the village of Omarakana in the Trobriand Islands" (Forge, 1972, p. 292). The ethnographer was to go forth to exotic places, live among the natives, partake of their hospitality and wisdom, and return in a year or so to "write up his notes" on "his people."

This archetype has been passed down in the "1:1:1 ratio—one man, one village, one year" (Hackenberg, 1993, p. 13). It is not only our legacy; many also believe it is the path into an uncertain future.

> Now as you start to focus your telescopes on the forbidding landscape before you, steady your hand with the knowledge that you stand in the shadow of the giants of the past. You are descended from a family of living legends. This is *your* turn to add *your* chapter. Remember, you are an anthropologist—the secret envy of those sociologists and economists down the hall. You get to go places and deal with people; they only get to stay here and mess with numbers. So, as you go about your exotic business, swagger a little. One of those almost forgotten giants might have muttered with ill-conceived disdain, and a heavy Polish accent, "Accountants die in bed." (Hackenberg, 1988, p. 184)

With the haughty humor of insiders, anthropologists have long referred to the solitary ethnographer as the "Lone Ranger." It is an apt personification. Ethnographers "earn their spurs" in the field and nowhere else. The Lone Ranger will forever be ethnography's culture hero, even though today we are just as likely to find he and Tonto at each other's throats as riding side by side into the sunset (Alexie, 1993). But who was that masked man, anyway? And was he really so all alone?

As it turns out, the Lone Ranger did not have "a heavy Polish accent." At least not the first one. And Roy Rogers might be a more fitting culture hero. Roy rode the range as well, but in the company of Dale Evans, the Sons of the Pioneers, Pat Brady atop the ever-sputtering Nellybelle, his dog Bullet, and, of course, Trigger (Yoggy, 1996, p. 163).

It was Frank Hamilton Cushing, not Malinowski, who "invented" participant observation when, in September 1879, he invited himself into the governor's house at Zuni—and stayed 4½ years (Green, 1990, p. 4). His was an anthropological sojourn still without equal. But Cushing has served ethnography more as object lesson than as exemplar, his name most often invoked in warnings of what can happen if the anthropologist "goes native" (Gronewold, 1972). So the first lone ranger ethnographer was really a pushy American from back East. He wasn't all alone, either. We forget, or never learn, that Cushing's research was carried out as part of the Bureau of American Ethnology's first southwestern expedition, under the direction of James Stevenson. Others in the party were photographer John Hillers and Stevenson's wife, Matilda, who would become Cushing's rival and outspoken critic in Zuni ethnography.

Abandoned to his own devices, his methods considered "absurd and ill-advised" by the Zunis and his associates alike, Cushing remained dependent on the Stevenson expedition for financial support and for communication with his superiors back at the Smithsonian (Green, 1990, p. 40). The Stevensons periodically conducted their own research at Zuni during Cushing's 4½-year stay, and Cushing was called on to assist others in their archaeological and ethnographic research elsewhere in the region (see the annual reports of the Bureau of Ethnology for 1881-1882 [Powell, 1884, pp. xiii-xxxvii] and 1882-1883 [Powell, 1886, pp. xxvii-xxviii]). After his Zuni fieldwork ended in 1884, Cushing went on to direct the Hemenway Southwestern Archaeological Expedition (from 1886 to 1888), which included Cushing's brother-in-law Frederick Hodge, historian Adolph Bandelier, three physical anthropologists (Washington Matthews, Herman F. C. ten Kate, and Jacob Wortman), an artist, and a publicist (Hinsley, 1983; Hinsley & Wilcox, 1996). This expedition not only laid the foundation for studies of the prehistoric Hohokam, it also "brilliantly anticipated modern strategies of multidisciplinary teamwork" (Hinsley & Wilcox, 1996, p. xv).

It was the expedition, not the independent investigator, that the first ethnographers chose as their research model when they got up out of their armchairs and went to the field. Like the Smithsonian's Bureau of Ethnology, the British Association for the Advancement of Science sponsored a series of expeditions during the late 19th and early 20th centuries, among them the Ethnographic Survey of the British Isles and the Torres Straits Expedition led by Alfred Cort Haddon.

Haddon's expedition to the Torres Straits, the islands between what is now Papua New Guinea and Australia, was designed as a team enterprise from the start. After an initial zoological visit to the Torres Straits, Haddon returned home in 1889, convinced of the need for ethnographic inquiry by a team that could transcend his own limitations. He wrote in his journal that "a proper anthropologist requires wider knowledge and more versatile talents than I can lay claim to. He should be a linguist, artist, musician and have an extensive knowledge of natural and mechanical science, etc." (quoted in Quiggin, 1942, p. 89). Besides linguists and musicologists, Haddon felt the need for professional insights into the minds of the islanders, and so he sought out W. H. R. Rivers, a psychologist then lecturing to the Cambridge Medical School. Rivers initially turned him down, and so Haddon looked elsewhere (pp. 95-96).

When two of Rivers' students, William McDougall and Charles Myers, signed on, Rivers changed his mind. In all, seven researchers, including a linguist and a photographer, embarked on March 10, 1898. Members of the Torres Straits Expedition came to be known as the "Cambridge School," the first generation of British anthropological fieldworkers.

Although they amassed an impressive set of publications over the next four decades (cf. Haddon, 1931), Stocking (1983) argues that "it was less the empirical data it collected than the expedition itself as a symbol of ethnographic enterprise that established the group's reputation" (p. 80). He quotes Haddon as saying "that 'two or three good men should always be in the field' supported by an international council that would set research priorities" (p. 81).

But the solitary investigator soon replaced the expedition as the dominant paradigm for ethnographic research. Two years before Malinowski set up his tent on Omarkana in 1915, Rivers had admonished ethnographers to work alone to avoid the "disturbance and excitement produced among natives by the various activities of the different members of an expedition" (quoted in Stocking, 1983, p. 92). Some years earlier, Rivers (1906) had "graduated" from being a member of Haddon's team to Lone Ethnographer among the Toda (Kuklick, 1996). By the time he made that statement, British-trained anthropologists already were conducting independent field studies in far-flung locations such as New Guinea, Bolivia, Siberia, the American Southwest, and the Pacific islands (Stocking, 1983, p. 83). It was not long before one (wo)man, one village was the order of the day.[2]

Nevertheless, the team has continued as a viable model of ethnographic research. Some team efforts are quite well known (even famous), others obscure; some have been highly successful, others have ended in failure. Among the better-known examples are several projects among the Navajo and surrounding groups including Clyde Kluckhohn's Ramah and Comparative Values in Five Cultures projects, 1936-1953, and Cornell University's projects at Many Farms and Fruitland, 1948-1961 (Lamphere,

1979); the Cornell-Peru Project (Vicos), 1952-1966 (Doughty, 1987); the Harvard Chiapas Project, 1957-1975 (Vogt, 1979); the Stirling County Study, 1948-1956 (Leighton, 1959); the Tri-Ethnic Project, 1959-1967 (Jessor, Graves, Hanson, & Jessor, 1968); the Kalahari Research Project, 1963-1976 (Lee, 1979); and the Changing Relations Project, 1988-1990, which used teams of ethnographers to study newcomers and established residents in six U.S. cities (Lamphere, 1992).

It is in applied research that ethnographers most often find themselves members of teams, usually multidisciplinary ones. Beginning in the 1920s, W. Lloyd Warner and his colleagues and students (including Elton Mayo, Eliot Chapple, Conrad Arensberg, Burleigh Gardner, and Solon Kimball) carried out two of the most influential team projects in social science—the Hawthorne and Yankee City studies (Partridge & Eddy, 1987).

One has only to scan the contents of *Human Organization*, *Practicing Anthropology*, *Anthropology and Education Quarterly*, or any of several collections of case studies in applied anthropology to note how embedded team research is in the doing of ethnography—and vice versa (Stull & Schensul, 1987). Indeed, applied anthropology offers an interesting contrast to "mainstream" outlets for basic research, or what Partridge and Eddy (1987) call "abstract anthropology" (pp. 5-7). Using single versus multiple authorship as a rough indicator of whether the research was done alone or in a team, we can compare the relative importance of teams for applied and abstract research. Representing abstract ethnography, we find that less than one fifth of the manuscripts submitted to the *Journal of Contemporary Ethnography* from 1986 to 1994 had multiple authors (Adler & Adler, 1995, p. 10); the Lone Ranger still rides ethnography's abstract range. Over the same period, however, 31% of the articles published in *Human Organization*, the leading international journal of applied anthropology, had two or more authors.

Whether the goals of the research were abstract or applied, team research has played an important role in ethnography. Nevertheless, very little has been written on the subject (see Fujisaka & Grayzel, 1978; Gow, 1991; and Perlman, 1970, for notable exceptions), and Rivers' preference for lone ethnography still is reproduced in texts on ethnographic and anthropological research methods (e.g., Bernard, 1994).

Despite the prevailing myth, today's ethnographers are as likely to work on a team as they are to go it alone. Rather than the traditions of our academic disciplines, research goals and contexts will largely dictate whose company the ethnographer keeps. Team composition will determine the scope and sphere of the ethnographer's responsibilities. Team dynamics are an integral, if not always explicit, part of the research process, and they will govern research outcomes to a great degree.

Margaret Mead once observed that "perhaps no other endogamous marriages . . . present quite as many hazards" as anthropological ones (Mead, 1970, p. 327). Nevertheless, the most common type of ethnographic team is the married couple, sometimes with children, more often without; sometimes both spouses are ethnographers, often not. Mead, in fact, twice entered the field as a member of husband-wife teams (first with Reo Fortune and later with Gregory Bateson) as well as in the company of another husband-wife team (Theodore and Lenora Schwartz).

Despite their ubiquity, we will set married teams aside. We lack the experience to discuss the issues, important as they are, that come with such territory. Those interested in married teams may wish to consult not only Mead (1970) and other contributors to *Women in the Field* (Golde, 1970) but also Firth (1972), Anderson (1990), Wax (1971), and Ward (1989). Tedlock (1995) presents a fascinating account of ethnographers' wives and the literature they have produced.

Age, sex, ethnicity, class, training, experience, inclination, and circumstance all play key roles in the field. They also influence our views of team research. The reader may have noticed from the title page that both of us are men—white guys at that. Our research has been carried out entirely within the United States. Neither of us has worked as a member of a married team, although we have been involved in teams that included married couples.

Both of us are anthropologists, and although ethnography is not owned by anthropology, we often act as if it were. In fact, team ethnography has drawn on the expertise of many disciplines from the very beginning. Although we will emphasize anthropological fieldwork and ethnographic research, we believe the matters we present and the lessons learned are salient to team research in general.

Research projects have life spans; so do research teams. Our discussion is organized according to the "typical" life course of team research, from inception to fieldwork to analysis, writeup, dissemination, and whatever afterlife may follow. We have worked in teams that included women, married couples, people of color, students, members of diverse professional training, community activists, and indigenous persons. We hope our experience, along with what we have learned from our colleagues in print and private, has alerted us to the many issues and perspectives in team research, but our discussion will no doubt be colored—some might say biased—by who we are and what we have seen and done. We will talk about both the "is" and the "ought," both the "real" and the "ideal." In the end, we hope to convince the reader that team research has an important place in fieldwork. Done right, it produces rich, comprehensive, trustworthy ethnography.

2. GETTING STARTED

Arrived in GC [Garden City] around 6:30 after driving like a wild man. Art Jose, and Michael were already here and after having a quick beer we met Janet and Ken at the Grain Bin. We had the first meeting in which all of us were in the same place at the same time. The team seems to have the right chemistry, and with the help of "good cow" and "good booze" we went 'til 11:00 p.m.

—Donald Stull (fieldnotes,
September 30-October 2, 1987)

Air service to Garden City, Kansas, was expensive, far too expensive for our as yet unfunded project. For out-of-town team members, the drive to this community on the High Plains took almost a full day, regardless of how adept the driver became at avoiding the few state troopers who waited for speeders on the long, empty two-lane roads leading into town. In Garden City, we shared the roads with pickup trucks, their rifles and catch ropes displayed in their rear windows, and with late-model "muscle cars" driven by the young men drawn to the relatively high hourly wages of the beefpacking plants. For all of us, driving into town required an olfactory adjustment to the constant background smells of the beef industry—dust, manure, offal—which, like the locals, we soon were calling "the smell of money."

Our first dinner together marked our adjustment to the field and to one another as well. Coming together over food marked a symbolic beginning. The steaks we ate had doubtless been killed, chilled, and boxed only a few days before by the people we had come together to study. Dinner table conversation, shared space, and shared food and drink were natural catalysts for a planned event, a small ritual to inaugurate our team. This beginning, like ethnographic teamwork anywhere, would activate existing relationships and explore new ones. Like all team beginnings, we negotiated the boundaries of our research territory, set goals and objectives, and created— or stumbled on—a manageable means to reach them.

Preparing for ethnographic fieldwork has been compared to the warmup for a dance performance (Janesick, 1994); stretching and practicing dance moves at the beginning are followed by similar moves during performance and cooldown. Design decisions made at the beginning—the stretching— should reflect the team's performance goals. Generating goals from an initial focus leads to negotiation about objectives and field tactics, determines who should be part of the team, and establishes an organizational framework to allow the team to take full and systematic advantage of ethnography's dance steps. Here, we discuss each in turn: involvement in an initial research focus by individuals who would make up a team, setting goals, team composition, and organizational issues.

The Changing Relations Project Team Focus

The Ford Foundation's launch of the Changing Relations Project (CRP) early in 1987, and the research focus that resulted, involved multiple views from the very beginning. The project grew from a desire within the Ford Foundation and among its collaborators to be ready for the 1990 census, a census that would show the greatest growth in new-immigrant population since the great wave of European immigration to the United States at the turn of the century (Bach, 1993). The project was administered by a team—a board of six social scientists, some of whom we knew by reputation. Each of us had heard of other anthropologists who were putting together proposals for other towns.

The CRP was designed to investigate "local-level interrelationships among new immigrants and established residents" in selected communities across the country. The project announcement required that fieldwork be carried out by ethnographic teams. The accompanying project statement indicated a preference for teams with on-site experience as well as ethnic and gender composition reflecting the study communities.

Several months before the Ford Foundation announced its intention to request project proposals for the CRP, Don Stull had visited Garden City, drawn by newspaper accounts of the paradox of Southeast Asian refugees in a small Kansas town. In response to the CRP announcement and preproposal invitation, Stull began assembling a team. He knew little about the community and even less about Southeast Asians, but the call for proposals dictated that he put together a team to study at least three distinct groups of newcomers and established residents. Stull had conducted ethnographic research in several Kansas communities and institutional contexts, so unfamiliarity with the specific composition of Garden City was balanced by a long-standing engagement with regional issues.

Stull was acquainted with Ken Erickson, then a practicing anthropologist and regional refugee services coordinator in Garden City. Michael Broadway, a social geographer at Wichita State University, had worked for Erickson on a study of the demographic characteristics and settlement patterns of Garden City's Southeast Asians and had served on his master's committee. Broadway agreed to join them. Erickson next recruited Janet Benson, an anthropologist from Kansas State University with research experience in multiethnic settings in India, who also had become interested in Garden City's refugee community. But a study of new-immigrant Southeast Asians would not satisfy the project's national board; certainly, there was more to Garden City's cultural mix than Southeast Asian newcomers and Anglo-American old-timers.

We soon learned that Garden City's established residents included not only long-established families who often called themselves "Mexican Americans" but also a rapidly growing population of Mexican and Central American immigrants. We needed someone with research experience among Spanish speakers but could find no one in our own institutions. Stull persuaded Art Campa, whom he had known since graduate school, to join up. Campa convinced the other members of the emerging team that they needed his colleague, Jose Cintron, to do ethnography in Garden City High School.

This was the group that met over drinks and steaks in Garden City's swankiest restaurant that September night. The team members came from four universities and a state social service agency. Only one lived in the study community; the rest were scattered over two states and 600 miles. Most barely knew each other, and some had never met. Yet, without ever coming together in one place until that night, they had put together a successful proposal, weathered a site visit, and landed one of six research contracts awarded by the CRP—the only one given for research in a small town in the Midwest (the other sites were Chicago, Houston, Miami, Philadelphia, and Monterey Park, a suburb of Los Angeles). For the next 2½ years, rarely would they all be together in one place at one time again, yet they saw the project through to completion. Team members continue to publish and otherwise disseminate their findings individually and collectively, and several have collaborated on new projects.

Setting Goals

Individual interests, histories, and identities were brought together by a common professional interest in changes in a High Plains community. An external push from the Ford Foundation provided a focus: newcomers and established residents. In part because Stull brought the proposal to the table, he was cast as the team leader; no one else seemed willing to audition for that part at the time.

We had to set out some research goals for ourselves and for our proposal to the foundation. In shaping the focus into goals, we discovered our capabilities and interests. Would we study just one town, or would it be better to compare Garden City to Dodge City, the archetypal cow town 50 miles to the east? Should we include Liberal, a packinghouse town an hour south, down on the Oklahoma state line? Should our lens be wide enough to include the schools as well as other public arenas of newcomer/ established-resident contact? Would our team—five men and one woman, four Anglos and two Latinos—be able to capture the points of view of both women and men? Of Southeast Asians, Mexicans, Mexican Americans, and established-resident "Gringos"? We talked at length of these matters as well as the more mundane, but no less vital, ones of budget, time lines, and individual responsibilities. Stull checked our emerging decisions against the project board's vision in phone calls as our proposal took shape. The CRP board directed us to limit our study to one community; it also insisted that we conceive our project as a study of "arenas" such as workplace and school.

In a community, in a corporate organization, or in any research site, someone always will ask, "So, just what is it you are doing, anyway?" Our team needed a comprehensible answer to this question, a way to represent itself to the community where it would be working. When an outside funding agency sets the focus, one might expect answers to the "What are you doing?" question to flow clearly and smoothly toward a shared research goal. Often this is not the case. Goals are either the negotiated products of team members' formal discussions or the informal collective results—the habitus—of their actions. When the team has multiple goals, members need to talk about their goals in ways that promote rather than discourage open communication about what is to be learned and why. Team members—and their project—have to be comprehensible not only to one another and their funders but also to the people with whom they interact.

If ethnography is about discovering—and creating—a story, then the narrative task at the beginning is to come up with a shared story that explains "what we are doing here." How this question is answered by the team will influence its members' ability to answer Agar's (1996) ethnographic question, "What is going on here?"

Setting our team's research goals was a balancing act. We were balancing our perceived differences against our perception of what the CRP board wanted, what the community could be expected to support (or tolerate), and what time, distance, and money would permit. Research teams, by joining diverse theoretical and empirical contributions of individual scholars with complementary skills, are especially well suited to basic research on big issues such as immigration, intergroup relations, and the structuring of ethnic diversity. Indeed, sponsoring institutions may expect teams to generate positive results by negotiating their conflicts into new perspectives, new empirical findings, and new theories about basic questions in the human sciences. The point about goal setting is, of course, that answers to "What are you doing?" do not emerge autochthonous from some mythological theoretical ground. They grow in a context of competing claims for attention and legitimacy, pushed in certain directions by the researchers, pruned a bit by the funders, and shaped by the field itself. The contest over goals results in negotiated answers to this question, answers that can guide the team in its decisions about its membership and its objectives.

Selecting Team Members

Project beginnings are experienced differently by different members of any team. Some teams, like the CRP-Garden City team, include strangers who may never have met until the project begins. Others are made up of colleagues who have worked together so often that they slide easily into their respective roles, like hands into comfortable old work gloves. Regardless of team members' levels of experience with one another, all new projects demand some sort of shakedown, some planning, and some interpersonal "stretching exercises."

When the team begins to fit a project's overall focus to a local context, ethnographers will discover the diversity in their interests and strengths. They will find that they have different approaches to the funding agency's focus and different views about what questions to ask. The discussions need to happen, the disagreements must be aired, and the tensions created by disciplinary, theoretical, or professional difference must be diffused, if not eliminated.

Riesman and Watson (1964) point out that "a multifaceted investigation can yield more information and be more exciting than one which is restricted to a single mode of knowing" (p. 286). But prior knowledge of one another, professional expertise, and an interesting research project are not enough. External exigencies, differences in personal style, theoretical and methodological disagreements, divided loyalties, competing professional demands, unclear lines of authority and responsibility, and unreasonable expectations of colleagues can frustrate achievement and cause lasting professional and personal rifts.

Such was the case with the Sociability Project, a 4-year study initiated by University of Chicago sociologists in 1954 to develop a theoretical framework for understanding sociable interaction (Riesman & Watson, 1964). Nelson Foote conceived the study and initiated it with David Riesman. Jeanne Watson was hired in 1955 as project director, and two male and two female graduate assistants were added from sociology, human development, and educational psychology. Despite substantial funding from the National Institute of Mental Health, the project broke apart on the rocks of difference. And teams must reconcile difference.

Like Haddon a century earlier, the CRP-Garden City team found itself lacking certain kinds of expertise. In particular, we needed someone who had worked with Mexican immigrant populations in the region. Like Haddon searching for a psychologist, the project struck paydirt. Seeking an ethnographer with Spanish-language skills, we got not one but two, and a school ethnographer in the bargain. A topic that might have seemed like "extra baggage" became an integral part of the research project. We had shied away from schools early on; integrating them not only improved our project, it allowed us to carry on in unexpected ways after we were through. Selecting team members, then, may redirect the trajectory of the research project.

We are the first to admit that team research often is beset by difficulty, especially if team members have not worked together before and come from disparate research traditions. Indeed, one of the six CRP teams was replaced midway through the project because of internal strife. We have experienced our share of acrimonious professional partings. More often, however, we have found new colleagues and built lasting friendships. Positive personal and professional relations are essential to successful long-term projects such as the Harvard Chiapas Project.

Invited in 1955 by Mexican anthropologists to evaluate Inter-American Indian Institute (INI) programs, Evon Vogt fell in love with the Chiapas highlands. With a small grant and a graduate assistant, he began research there in the summer of 1957. In 1975, 20 years after he first visited the region, the Harvard Chiapas Project had provided research experience for 136 fieldworkers and produced 27 monographs, 100 scholarly articles, and 21 doctoral dissertations (Vogt, 1979).

Multidisciplinary teams that have never worked together before are common in applied research, especially technical assistance projects. When government agencies or private corporations call on social scientists, as often as not they are there to find ways to "correct" errors in policies or programs. Perils endemic to such projects include professional bigotry, and ethnographers often find themselves needing to continually prove their worth not only to employers but also to the more "scientific" of their teammates such as economists, animal scientists, or plant scientists. Personal conflict often goes hand in hand with professional conflict, inadequate division of labor and delegation of authority, and client unwillingness to accept "uncomfortable knowledge" (Gow, 1991).

Ethnographers increasingly find themselves working alongside colleagues from other backgrounds. Whether a "hired gun" or one among other scholarly investigators, team building is essential. Expertise, research experience, and compatibility are the keys to project success (Gow, 1991, p. 11), but the greatest of these probably is compatibility. Compatibility often is discovered in the course of research. New friendships are made, and old ones sometimes are broken, in team projects. Investigators find out (often the hard way) who they can work with and who will deliver the goods (and deliver them on time). Dependability is thus a vital component of compatibility.

In his analysis of teamwork in development consulting, David Gow (1991) distinguishes between musketeers and stooges: "Musketeers are performers par excellence. . . . Stooges . . . can only survive as members of teams where others will cover up for their mistakes and failures" (p. 10). Musketeers are the colleagues you will call on the next time; you work with stooges only once.

The Organizational Structure

Some teams clearly are bounded and hierarchical; others are alliances of fieldworkers working on individual projects with the same or related groups and writing up findings separately. Some teams have general open-ended research questions; others, like the CRP, address questions that are specified beforehand in a research contract. The loose alliance has been the model of most team ethnography since the 1940s (Sanjek, 1990, p. 330). Kluckhohn's Ramah Project is among the better known examples of an alliance investigating loosely related research questions (Lamphere, 1979, pp. 22-28). This study of a community of several hundred Navajo south of Gallup, New Mexico, ran from 1939 to 1948, when it was incorporated into a new team project, the Comparative Study of Values in Five Cultures, a comparison of native and non-native communities in the Ramah area. Alexander and Dorothea Leighton and other psychiatrists, psychologists, and physicians, as well as 15 graduate students in anthropology, were associated with Kluckhohn on this project. Team members were but loosely affiliated and pursued their own interests and publications.

15

Not that ethnographers are anarchists. But they are trained in a lone ranger tradition that does not provide experience in giving—and taking—direction in the field. This could be seen as a natural byproduct of an inductive stance that resists fixing goals and methods too early in the research process. The team's structure, whether formal and hierarchial or diffuse and egalitarian, is influenced by the relative status of its members. Investigators of similar professional status and age may balk at formalized organizational structure, narrowly defined roles, and outside imposition of research questions. Whatever the underlying causes, we found leadership to be a difficult issue for the CRP.

One of our efforts to formalize our team's organizational structure was the CRP-Garden City Team Compact. Drafted from an example provided by Roger Sanjek, it was concerned not only with sorting out ahead of time how we would deal with our "rights" to project data and our access to one another's fieldnotes. The written compact, reproduced here from the CRP-Garden City project files, also hinted at a more formal organizational structure than what ultimately came to life.

This project is a joint venture, intended to be both cooperative and collaborative. Its overall goal is to answer the research questions contained in the "Changing Relations Project Statement." Each team member is expected to participate in project meetings and related activities and to carry out research according to the plan set forth in the research proposal, "Changing Relations in a High Plains Boomtown," as amended and augmented by associated documents. Team members will provide regular financial reports, research reports, briefing papers, and other such documents as called for in the prime contract and subcontracts and as may be needed to successfully complete the overall project goals.

All information will be collected, stored, analyzed, and reported in such a way as to protect the identity, privacy, and integrity of informants and community collaborators. Confidentiality and anonymity will be guaranteed to all respondents unless explicitly waived, and quotes attributed to named individuals will be shared with them prior to publication. However, intrateam communication requires that fieldnotes and interview transcriptions bear proper identification, except in extremely delicate and pressing situations.

Data collected under the sponsorship of this project, including each person's fieldnotes and interview tapes/transcriptions, belong to the team member who collects them. At the same time, all data collected specifically for the project (excluding individual fieldnotes and interviews) are the joint property of all team members. Project members are expected to make the data they collect (including fieldnotes, interview transcriptions, documents, photographs, etc.)

available in the Garden City office in a timely fashion. Team members are free to use the data they collect for publications. They may also use other project data to supplement their own. Data in fieldnotes may be used by other team members only if the person who produced the fieldnotes consents and full acknowledgment is given.

All team members are free to publish or disseminate data and analyses from the project, subject to restrictions set forth in the prime contract, provided that they (1) acknowledge project sponsorship and project members who collected any data other than their own; and (2) circulate prepublication drafts of any publications, papers, or analyses to other team members, with sufficient time for review and comment. Royalties from publications or sale of photographs belong to the author, but other team members may use any photographs in their professional activities.

General guidelines for authorship/acknowledgment are as follows: (1) all team members with a possible interest in a particular topic are invited to become coauthors; (2) only those persons who actually participate in the writing of a publication will be listed as coauthors; (3) authors are listed in order of the magnitude of their contributions; and (4) where the contributions of coauthors are considered equal, authors are listed in alphabetical order. Publications that draw upon data collected by someone who does not participate in the writing process should recognize that person's contribution in an acknowledgment.

Team members who wish to collect data that are not directly related to the stated research goals shall present their requests to the rest of the team for their approval.

Basic decisions concerning the project will be made at regularly scheduled team meetings, which all team members are expected to attend. In other circumstances, all team members will be polled on major decisions.

* * *

Designing a structure can take place around a conference table, but putting a structural design into practice is another matter. We put some of our team compact into practice, but not all of it and not all of the time. We found it difficult to gather the entire team together for regular meetings, and we continually wrestled with the conflicting demands that family, work, and the field make on all ethnographers. Meeting the letter of the compact often seemed beyond our corporate reach. Meeting the corporate spirit of a compact like this one is a continual challenge, especially for the team leader who, more than anyone else, is responsible for making a team project out of individual effort.

It takes time to deal with the administrative details, to ferret out and transmit what researchers are learning on their own, and to make the findings part of a team's emerging understanding of the field experience. For a team leader, project management draws effort away from research in the field. Time spent by the team leader in solo fieldwork amounts to time not spent on preliminary comparisons among team-collected data, team meetings, and getting to know the team itself. A team will suffer in its ability to come to a shared understanding of its emerging findings if it lacks a systematic way of attending to team management. Here, teams may come to adopt management structures ranging from hierarchical to egalitarian.

Hierarchical teams, like the team of researchers who produced the Yankee City study, consist of a senior principal investigator and a cadre of fieldworkers, commonly graduate students. Such efforts often are directed by a principal investigator who stays home at the museum, the university, or the research and consulting firm. The principal investigator also may oversee a "home team" that processes fieldnotes, aggregates the data, and fires off memoranda or summary questionnaires to fieldworkers. Griaul (1957, p. 25) called this design the "double team" approach. In it, one team has access to a social world in the field; the other stays home, with access to comparative material and time to provide external critique and analysis.

Steward (1956) used this technique when he sent ethnographers to investigate the varieties of human adaptation to different ecological and historical environments in Puerto Rico. According to Robert Manners, one of the team members, notes were too many and logistics too difficult for the individual fieldworkers to review one another's notes while in the field (Erickson, 1989).

Teams may find that hierarchical organizations make sense in some settings but not in others. The key is that there must be some clear sense of organization. Newer teams might do better with more directive, hierarchical leadership. Established teams may be able to get along without this style of organization, but they will not get along without some regular systematic means of bringing together the team's individual observations and diverse approaches.

Competent, compatible, experienced multidisciplinary teams, such as the Kalahari Research Project (Lee, 1979), have had a major impact on theoretical development in the social sciences. The world needs the perspectives ethnographic teams can bring; negotiating the goals, the team composition, and organizational structure of the team are necessary steps along the road.

3. GETTING THERE—TOGETHER

Because the aim of fieldwork is to encompass a whole, and as many parts of that whole in as much detail as possible, field teams are successful to the extent that the skills and capacities, temperaments and interests of the team members are complementary, asymmetrical, and noncompetitive.

—Margaret Mead (1970, p. 326)

When the stretching is over, the real business of fieldwork begins. Research teams are supposed to be just that—teams. Members should have clear and complementary responsibilities, and mechanisms should be in place to share observations and interpretations. But too often teammates slip into solitary ways despite their own best intentions and the efforts of project directors. When this happens, project findings are likely to be attenuated and project outcomes unsatisfactory. Even worse, teams may break up prematurely and projects may self-destruct, causing long-standing fissures in professional relationships.

Systematic sharing of observations and regular ongoing interpretation of their meanings are essential to successful team research. Observations may be shared in several ways. One way is that observers may witness the same event and then discuss it afterward. Second, investigators may read each other's fieldnotes and offer comments, add information, or challenge interpretations. A third way is that teams can hold regular debriefing sessions to present and analyze members' findings.

Seeing the Same Thing Differently

A second experiment was conducted in which four staff members of the Sociability Project attended the same party and all took notes, retiring periodically to a back room set up for this purpose. They found, as might have been expected, that they did not attend the "same party." (Riesman & Watson, 1964, p. 299)

Team members are commonly assigned to different sites and different arenas of observation. After all, teams usually want to maximize their coverage of people and events. But at times, it may be advantageous for more than one observer—perhaps the whole team—to witness an event.

Gender, ethnicity, theoretical orientation, and experience influence what investigators see and how they interpret it. As Rosaldo (1993) put it,

> All interpretations are provisional; they are made by positioned subjects who are prepared to know certain things and not others. Even when knowledgeable, sensitive, fluent in the language, and able to move easily in an alien cultural world, good ethnographers still have their limits, and their analyses always are incomplete. (p. 8)

This being the case, two heads (or more) should be better than one, especially when opportunities for observation are limited. Meatpacking executives declined to participate in our study of ethnic relations in Garden City. Denied regular access to plant floors, we interviewed workers and managers and hung out with them in their favorite bars, read trade journals, and attended monthly workers' compensation hearings. We also became adept at finagling our way onto plant tours, which management offers to groups it considers friendly or at least nonthreatening (e.g., chambers of commerce, stockmen and stockwomen, the Future Farmers of America).

Modern meatpacking plants are a wondrous conflagration of meat, machines, and (wo)men—crosscut by linguistic and cultural difference. To spend an hour or so on their floors is an unforgettable experience, one that attacks the senses and boggles the mind (Stull, 1994). Short, sporadic, and controlled periods in the plants result in only partial, and often erroneous, information. As a corrective measure, members of our team went on plant tours together as often as possible, followed by tape-recorded debriefing sessions. Such sessions enabled each of us to fill in gaps in our own knowledge base, correct false impressions, and engage in preliminary analyses. Invariably, each one of us saw, or did not see, different things— and our interpretations of what we did see sometimes differed.

Donald Stull: Tony [our guide] said . . . they start at 7:00 in the morning and go to 4:00 p.m., and then the next shift starts at 4:00 and goes to about 1:00 a.m.

Janet Benson: 12:30 a.m.

Art Campa: My informant said 12:45.

Stull: The people I know that work at Monfort, they come in invariably earlier to Tom's [Tavern] than do the IBP people. [Monfort and IBP are the two beef plants in Garden City; Tom's Tavern was a favorite hangout for beefpacking workers.] . . . The guy I know best is a beef lugger, and he's always there before midnight. . . . There are other people who come in that are Monfort people. They seem to come in earlier. It may just be the particular jobs they have.

Benson: Yeah, they are closer, but they're coming in 15 or 20 minutes before the IBP people, so it's not a question of just how far they have to drive. It's clear that not everybody gets off at the same time.

Campa: I was told that some are staggered, like at intervals of 15 minutes. Like Raoul and Francisco, let's see, one starts at 4:15, the other starts at 5:00. And they work anywhere from 32 to 40 hours a week. Management tries not to let them work overtime if they are whitehats [hourly workers].

Stull: Well, they have a guarantee of 32 hours a week. . . . Most of them have not, at least this winter, been working more than they're guaranteed. And I saw a sign that indicated that the guarantee for the weekend was suspended.

Benson: I noticed some things about gender. I was looking for women in the various operations; I noticed there was a woman in the security office; there were two male officers there. There were some women in Slaughter, but they were at sinks over on the side. Most of the people at the boning table were male, but there were some women boning. I'm not sure what to think of some of Tony's statements, but I thought they were interesting. He made the statement that in the case of married workers, it was common to find that the wife has a job at one plant on one shift and the husband has a job at another plant on a different shift. That way, they cover the child care because they want to avoid the expense of child care. Now, if that is a common pattern in that plant, then it may differentiate Hispanics from Vietnamese because, in my experience, although some Vietnamese do that, it's not very common, and it is common for both husband and wife to work at the same plant on the same shift, and they usually find child care among neighbors or members of the Vietnamese community.

Stull: Well, he also pointed out that they start late because that's what their workers prefer; it gives more time to arrange things in the morning, and one of the rationales he gave for the roughly 1-hour difference between IBP and Monfort in start-up and closing times was to allow that kind of coordination between spouses. I suspect that's probably rationalization.

Benson: And then the other statement he made that was interesting was about his feeling that if women didn't do particular jobs, it was because they had a mind-set about not being able to do them, and he stated that all the jobs could be done by either sex. I find that hard to believe. (CRP-Garden City team debriefing of March 17, 1989, tour of Monfort beef plant, recorded March 18, 1989)

Debriefing

As the preceding interchange illustrates, debriefing can clear up confusion over cultural details. More important, such sessions can tease out underlying cultural themes and enrich analytical perspectives. Regularly scheduled—and structured—debriefing sessions maximize intrateam communication and ensure that researchers stay on task and on schedule. Bohannan (1981, pp. 36-39) used debriefing to maximum effect in a study of nonwelfare senior citizens living in single-room occupancy hotels (SROs) in downtown San Diego. As principal investigator of the Unseen Community project, Bohannan did relatively little ethnographic research himself. Most of the field observations were carried out by four investigators who joined the team over a 3-year period.

Regular debriefing sessions began immediately and continued throughout the fieldwork. At intervals ranging from 3 days to 3 weeks, depending on the stage in the research, fieldworkers met with the principal investigator. They reviewed their notes in detail, and the principal investigator questioned them. Richer description emerged as fieldworkers explained what was in their notes and responded to probes from the principal investigator and other fieldworkers. Questions directed at the fieldworkers and their fuller explanations could lead to new insight—or the abandonment of "wrong-headed notions." New lines of inquiry came out of fieldworkers' inability to answer questions from the principal investigator.

The debriefing sessions enabled Bohannan to formulate questions about the theoretical significance of certain data while fieldworkers were investigating their importance for those who lived in the SROs. Debriefing sessions thus served to institutionalize the ongoing preliminary analysis that characterizes all ethnography—or should. As Bohannan points out, debriefing sessions are unnecessary for lone ethnographers, who question themselves in their heads and in their notes. For research teams, debriefings offer a greater sense of purpose than either informal meetings or occasional seminars. Structured interaction among and between team members brings different minds together to think about the same data or event. Such sessions also keep team members in touch with both the data and theory *while they are in the field.*

Occasionally, other social scientists or informants joined the Unseen Community project as guest debriefers. The team found their fresh insights and questions helpful. Bringing informants to these sessions did not work so well, however. They usually were uncomfortable with the analytic discussions and jargon of the investigators. (See Chapter 4 for another example of a "subject" becoming uncomfortable in a debriefing session, although for quite a different reason.)

Sessions were tape-recorded and initially transcribed in full. Full transcription was soon replaced by compact notes, which Bohannan annotated from the tapes. This extra procedure eliminated small talk and other irrelevant content from the transcripts while allowing participants to interact without worrying about the relevance of their every comment. More important, Bohannan's annotated notes differed from those of the fieldworkers, containing not only data but also working hypotheses, suggestions for further inquiry, and preliminary analyses.

Bohannan annotated the taped sessions himself and indexed the resulting transcripts. The task was dull, he admits, but also essential if he was to craft the findings of others into coherent project reports. He likens this task to indexing a book. Headings were transferred to cards; sometimes these headings were written in transcript margins, sometimes not. Bohannan indexed transcripts every 3 or 4 months. In so doing, he forced himself to periodically reread the annotated transcripts and thereby keep their content fresh in his mind. New headings were added as they emerged from the data, and basic information on each category was compiled into "subject sheets."

Bohannan (1981) reminds us that "it is necessary to go over . . . notes and . . . transcripts several times, at several months' intervals, so that new ideas can be worked through and old ideas rescued and all of it fitted together into a continually expanding view of the total problem" (p. 39). Such indexing is common among ethnographers; however, when working alone, they usually do it after leaving the field. In team research, it is not only possible but actually preferable to begin processing and analyzing data in the field. Ethnographers working together can use preliminary analyses—such as debriefing, compiling compact notes, and indexing—to check on and expand their findings, enhancing both the reliability and the validity of their team's research.

Making and Sharing Fieldnotes

Before any of us could write unconcealed reports of the sociability of ourselves—not to mention our husbands, wives, and dating partners—we had to be able to *like* and *trust* our colleagues who would read the reports. (Riesman & Watson, 1964, p. 269, emphases in original)

Fieldnotes are the first written products of a field team's ethnographic gazes. The plural, gaz*es*, sounds strange, but final reports from team ethnography are jointly constructed—or should be. Investigators unaccustomed to working together—or with others in general—often are protective of their notes. At first blush, reading and commenting on each other's fieldnotes would seem like a simple matter. All too often, that is not the case. Ethnographers frequently resist sharing notes, or, if forced to do so, they may produce two sets—an official set for public consumption and a private set of "real" notes. Social scientists without a tradition of note taking (e.g., survey researchers, demographers) often are reluctant to even attempt fieldnotes, and then they may be embarrassed by their paucity or crudeness (see Gibson, 1987, pp. 112-113).

Jean Jackson interviewed 70 anthropologists about fieldnotes and fieldnote taking. For ethnographers, especially those who work in teams, she offers a crucial cautionary tale. What Jackson's (1990) informants defined as a "fieldnote" varied widely, no doubt because most had received no formal training in fieldnote taking (pp. 6-8). As a result, "interviewees [were] very touchy on the topic of sharing notes" (p. 8). The reasons for such reluctance are many, but Jackson believes defensiveness about the quality of one's notes, and thus one's very work, is a root cause (p. 19). In fact, when rereading their notes, several anthropologists in Jackson's sample were disappointed with them.

For lone ethnographers, fieldnotes serve as *aides mémoir*, initial analyses, and archives to be visited when away from the field. For team ethnographers, fieldnotes are all these things and more; they also are a means to share findings with other team members. Unfortunately, anxiety about the adequacy of one's own notes and professional competition and jealousy combine with this tradition of secrecy to inhibit sharing of notes and thus the flow of information. As one of Jackson's (1990) informants put it, "The irony in anthropology is that [because fieldnotes are private,] we're really exercising acts of faith a lot of the time" (p. 30). This is bad enough when ethnographers work alone; it can cripple, or even destroy, team projects.

Like conversation, effective use of fieldnotes among two or more persons depends on certain shared conditions; trust is chief among them. Singh, Lele, and Martohardjono (1988) note that whenever speakers apply the "principle of humanity" (i.e., whenever they trust one another), they find ways around miscommunication. In other words, people can and do transcend different linguistic codes and interpersonal styles (Giles & Coupland, 1991). Likewise, ethnographers have different styles of working and writing. It takes time to build the trust necessary to bridge these differences, to learn what to expect from other team members, and to respond adequately to their needs and those of the project. Building trust is made more difficult by the walls of propriety ethnographers erect around fieldnotes. These walls of secrecy stand on foundations of "Malinowskian myth . . . and post-1960 individual grant practice" (Sanjek, 1990, p. 329). Sanjek goes on to remind us that until recently

there have been more Argonauts than Jasons. Fieldwork in the classical period was less Odyssey than Iliad, organized in programs, projects, schemes, and teams, with larger purposes than those envisioned in single-investigator research design. . . . *Fieldnotes were shared.* (p. 329, emphasis added)

But establishing a tradition of fieldnote sharing may be limited by the structure of the research team, and the circulation of notes varies according to project organization. It may be easier, at least on paper, for hierarchical teams to circulate their findings. For example, the 18 fieldworkers involved in the Yankee City study all submitted copies of their notes, as well as weekly reports, to the project director, W. Lloyd Warner. Fieldworkers had access to everyone else's fieldnotes and reports, although it was Warner who wrote up the results (Sanjek, 1990, p. 330).

Diffuse and egalitarian teams, the model of most team ethnography since the 1940s (Sanjek, 1990, p. 330), can and do share fieldnotes as well. Despite the large number of players and diversity of research agendas in the Comparative Study of Values in Five Cultures, researchers did cooperate in collecting certain data (e.g., psychological tests) and shared their fieldnotes. Kluckhohn (1944) drew on the fieldnotes of many project participants for his classic study of *Navaho Witchcraft*.

Writing fieldnotes for a team audience directs more explicit attention to the contextual features that inform the researcher's emergent analysis. Not only should notes be shared, but what is shared should be comprehensive. What Sanjek (1990) calls scratch notes—the contents of pocket notebooks and the rough outlines hacked onto a computer at dawn after an all-night ceremony—are fine working tools. They will not help other team members understand what was going on, however, until they are fleshed out and made part of the team's growing understanding.

For the lone ethnographer, the encounter with "the other" is the liminal part of the fieldwork rite of passage. Ethnographers who work in teams experience a double encounter: themselves, the "other," and the other researchers. This sets team members up for a double whammy. This double encounter is especially apparent when sharing fieldnotes. Ethnographers used to using notes only as rough mnemonic devices will find their notes inadequate. When the notes of a "lone ranger" are too sparse, team members ought to tell the writer that he or she is "telegraphing." Chances are, the author of such notes also will find them lacking when it comes time to write the final report or to use them in a publication 2 or 3 years down the line.

By the end of the project, fieldnotes should consistently communicate the researcher's experience and initial analysis to other members of the team. What's more, investigators learn to trust the other team members and build goodwill by reading and questioning each other's fieldnotes.

Sharing notes, then, requires an agreement to do so at the beginning. It requires enriched contextual content and a corporate understanding of who "owns" fieldnotes, who has access to them after the field excursion, and for what purposes. Explicit attention to this in the early going can set the stage for the transition from individual ethnographers who "own" their own notes to team members who share corporate ownership of the insights and analyses produced by the field encounters.

Where team members expect their fieldnotes to be read, the notes themselves can take on the character of reports or memoranda. Written for the usual purposes, such notes also are written to be read and to elicit responses, such as the following fragment from a study we conducted of shop floor relations in a meatpacking plant (Erickson, 1996; Stull, Erickson, & Giner, 1996).

> Most Spanish spoken at the plant is "Tex-Mex," and this has caused some translation problems. They found they had to have the written materials translated into the vernacular by local people. . . . *Translation could be inadequate. Miguel, Ken need to go over these materials to see how they read.* (memorandum from Donald Stull to Miguel Giner and Ken Erickson, August 31, 1994, emphasis in original)

Giner and Erickson, the Spanish-speaking members of our team, did indeed go over the translations—plenty of them. They developed a research strategy to understand how written and spoken translation took place in the plant, combining audio recordings, photographs, and team debriefings with their fieldnotes. We not only *shared* fieldnotes, we *used* each other's notes to direct our inquiry (Erickson, 1995).

Good Intentions Are
Not Enough

Ethnographers are socialized to the field. It anchors our identity (Kleinman & Coop, 1993, p. 19). We are passionate about fieldwork—in love with it. At least we think we are supposed to be. Even so, it is inordinately demanding—for many all-consuming—of time, energy, intellect, and psyche. To paraphrase Nathaniel Hawthorne: Fieldwork is damned hard work!

Fieldwork is stressful, whether you love it or merely pretend you do Tension is bound to run high from time to time; when strong-willed, solitary-minded professionals are thrown together, eruptions are inevitable.

Teams are fragile. Team building must not stop when everyone is on board and fieldwork gets underway. And compacts must be remembered and respected if they are to benefit teams and their individual members. A number of factors can hamper, if not undermine, team research goals and effectiveness.

CULT OF INDIVIDUALISM

Riesman and Watson (1964) blame "the cult of individualism" for many of the problems of the Sociability Project. They could just as easily have been speaking of ethnographic research in general when they wrote,

> The Sociability Project existed within a milieu which stressed the importance of creative achievement by individuals. . . . When our research encountered failure or difficulty, the responses had the character of guilt and blame rather than rational problem-solving. When an individual did have the glimmerings of a new idea, he was highly possessive and protective; if it amounted to anything, it was to be "his baby," and he did not want it stolen from him or made over by others—most especially not by the project directors. (pp. 270-271)

The Lone Ranger still rides. And all too often, alone, even when in the company of others. "Rugged individualism" is, after all, the Code of the West. Individualism also is a core value in academia. Initiation into its cult is the price of professional (wo)manhood. For no academic enterprise is this truer than ethnography; fieldwork is the ethnographer's rite of passage, and, like initiation rites among so many of those we study, the initiate must suffer and survive alone. The lessons learned of individualism are learned well. Individualism is more than a cult; it is the state religion of ethnography.

PROFESSIONAL COMPETITION

"Rugged individualism" helped "tame" the West; it also builds academic careers. Team members usually are selected for the particular skills they bring to the group; members' contributions often overlap, but each member is supposed to make a unique contribution—in disciplinary or methodological expertise, in language skills, in contacts with agencies or host populations. In other words, each member of the team should fill a niche; it may be topical, or it may be determined by linguistic or cultural expertise (Lee, 1979, p. 309). Division of labor, often quite discrete, should minimize, if not eliminate, jealousy and competition among team members. Often it does not, as the following excerpt from Stull's fieldnotes demonstrates.

I have now been back in GC [Garden City] for six weeks, and I feel like I have accomplished very little—not a single interview; some good conversations and notes, but nothing to brag about. I feel like Mark [Grey] and Art are even passing me by—there's no doubt their connections are deeper and more productive than mine. I've got to turn it around, but I still find it hard to figure out how to develop better contacts with the Anglos—they are friendly, but so hard to get beyond surface relationships. (Donald Stull, fieldnotes, January 27-February 20, 1989)

There are yardsticks ethnographers use to measure success in the field: number of interviews, "rapport" with their hosts, headway on their research problem. Their reference point usually is some goal—often vague—they set for themselves (see Rose, 1990, p. 35). But when they are part of a team, ethnographers have others' progress to measure against their own—and they do not always like what they find.

Different working styles and lifestyles, theoretical and methodological disputes, personal idiosyncrasies and overblown egos, or simply too much time in the company of one another all can lead to occasional flare-ups—and worse. Such differences often are exaggerated in interdisciplinary technical assistance or evaluation projects, as Gow (1991) found in a rural development project he directed in Panama.

The livestock specialist had a large and sensitive ego, and two-thirds of the way through the design effort, he felt [that] his contribution had been slighted and that the government had double-crossed him. Sobbing piteously, he maintained that the best thing for him to do would be to leave on the next plane. With a few encouraging strokes from other team members, however, his momentary loss of self-confidence was soon restored and he continued to play an important role in the design effort. More serious were the problems created by the first economist. Three days prior to the team's departure from the U.S., the original economist selected had called off, and we had scrambled desperately to find a replacement. The latter's résumé was impressive, but his performance was embarrassingly bad—both in terms of substance and in his relationships with the Panamanians. (p. 4)

Despite its name, the Sociability Project proved to be anything but. "The project came to be a 'tight little island' locked in internecine warfare" (Riesman & Watson, 1964, p. 256).

Anxiety was high; defensiveness was created by the many criticisms of the Sociability Project from colleagues both inside and outside the project, as well as from subjects. Each person felt that he had been placed in an untenable position by the actions of others on the project, and the resulting tensions and antagonisms within the project staff were disruptive. Eventually, alliances developed and factions were established. (p. 265)

FACTIONALISM

Individualism can destroy research teams; so can factionalism. Multi-disciplinary teams are subject to rifts along disciplinary or methodological borders. Fissures also may develop if members do not pull their weight or get their work in on time. Personal slights or professional criticisms, real or imagined, may fester and eventually become open sores. Cliques can form, and members can be excluded by dint of gender or ethnic difference, family obligations, or degree of sociability. Divisions between senior and junior staff can become serious problems, especially if senior staff are not in agreement and send mixed signals.

In part, this resulted from differences among top staff members with respect to what they wanted done; in part, it arose from inadequate explanation by top staff members to the assistants. . . . Eventually, these early events came to be seen as evidence of betrayal by the top staff, and a barrier of mistrust was established between assistants and their supervisors. . . . The assistants were divided from one another by attitudes of defensiveness and mutual suspicion.

The top staff members were unhappy about the growing antagonism from the assistants, but they had different explanations for it and different remedies. (Riesman & Watson, 1964, pp. 273-274)

MY PEOPLE, YOUR PEOPLE

Factionalism also can emerge from divided loyalties, which may emerge as ethnographers begin to identify with "their people." Not only was the Sociability Project beset by problems from within, it also had to cope with a divided team whose members felt they owed allegiance to their research subjects, not their teammates.

The researcher finds himself responding to his "subjects" as friends and allies. When, in addition, as on our project, he is separated from his colleagues by barriers of mistrust and anxiety, he finds himself in the peculiar situation of being identified with his subjects and against his colleagues.... The researcher himself does not want to "betray" his friends into his colleagues' hands. (Riesman & Watson, 1964, p. 266)

So-called native ethnographers normally are seen as "insiders" whose understanding of the host community is authentic—more authentic, in fact, than understandings available to non-native ethnographers (Narayan, 1993, p. 676). Research efforts such as the Changing Relations Project have sought to match the ethnicity of researchers and host communities (Lamphere, 1992). The dichotomy between "native" and "non-native" ethnographers is a dangerous one for ethnographic research in general (Narayan, 1993), however, and for multiethnic research teams in particular.

Ethnographers may find themselves disagreeing over what they see and what it means more because of their own ethnic identity than because of the verity of their data. Native ethnographers, as insiders, can become embroiled in the political agendas and factional disputes of "their people." Insider/outsider disputes may stimulate useful interpretive debates. They also may degenerate into petty games of one-upmanship.

The team that conducted the Punjabi Education Project, a collaborative research project designed to improve educational opportunities for Punjabis in "Valleyside," California, was made up of both insiders and outsiders to the study community, mixed by age, sex, ethnicity, and educational background (Gibson, 1987). The project director was an "American" anthropologist, Margaret Gibson; her coinvestigator was a Sikh with a background in educational research and evaluation. They were assisted by three insider and one outsider Punjabis as well as one "Valleysider." The

Punjabi assistants were assigned to interview friends and relatives, but complaints about the interviews and criticisms of their motives led one assistant to resign.

The project was jeopardized when the Punjabi coinvestigator became the focal point of a political dispute among Punjabi factions. Indeed, he was the leader of one of two warring factions within the community service agency that administered the project grant. This dispute eventually was "dampened" and the project continued, but Gibson and her Punjabi coinvestigator could not agree on "an approach to data analysis and report presentation. Since most of the analysis had to be done on [their] own time and in different locations," they reluctantly decided to submit separate reports to the funding agent, the school, and community members. When the local school district did not approve the coinvestigator's report, he accused them of being unwilling to "face and discuss the issues." The school district "found the coinvestigator's presentation regarding prejudice in the schools unsubstantiated and biased" (Gibson, 1987, p. 114).

RESEARCH HEADMEN—
RELUCTANT LEADERS

Administrative inexperience, often combined with reluctance to lead, are common problems for research teams. Academics by and large do not like structured work settings and often rebel against hierarchy. They expect their students to follow their lead, of course, and they do not mind telling them what to do. But taking orders from an "equal" (another Ph.D. researcher) is a different matter altogether. So is giving orders to one.

Authority and leadership among social research teams usually are "informal," much as they were among the Plains Indians during the 19th century. Among the Blackfeet, for example, a chief's power stemmed from his personal influence and charisma. Others followed him only so long as it suited them; they could change allegiance or ignore his authority if they wished (Oliver, 1974, p. 314). For most research teams, it is the same.

Blackfeet headmen of old had to hunt and make war as well as lead. Not until they proved themselves in the chase and on the field of battle would others listen to them. So it is on the field of team research. Researchers will not follow someone without a "proven track record." And team leaders, like their tribal counterparts, must continue to validate their position by performance (Oliver, 1974, p. 319).

Team administrators also usually think of themselves as researchers first, administrators second. They generally would rather be doing interviews, going to ceremonies, or hanging out than pouring over budgets, filing reports, or "riding herd" on team members. More often than not, they find themselves trying to fit their own research in between administrative duties. They do so not only because they enjoy research—reputations are built on publications. For ethnographers, publications derive from fieldwork, not from pushing paper and cracking whips.

Laura Thompson found herself in such a situation when she coordinated the Indian Education Research Project, a comparative study of the Papago, Hopi, Navajo, Zuni, and Dakota Sioux (Thompson, 1970). The project began in September 1941, shortly before the United States entered World War II, and was staffed primarily by women. Joining Thompson were anthropologist Ruth Underhill, psychiatrists Alice Joseph and Dorothea Leighton, and prominent consultants such as Ruth Benedict, Margaret Mead, Clyde Kluckhohn, Kurt Lewin, A. I. Hallowell, Fred Eggan, and Erik H. Erickson. Most of the fieldwork, however, was conducted by assistants living in the study communities such as teachers, nurses, and tribal members. The project ran for 6 years and included 150 workers, of whom 75 worked in the field.

In addition to her own research, which centered on the Hopi, Thompson (1970) managed the overall project's "fieldwork, data processing and comparison, interpretation, application, and reporting . . . [with] persistence, fortitude, and humor" (p. 57). She also had to coordinate and integrate alternate and sometimes incompatible theoretical and disciplinary approaches. "The fact that ideological differences are often interpreted as personal incompatibilities, especially by pragmatic American academicians, did not help" (p. 59). These differences were accommodated as the findings from the different disciplines and methods were presented and discussed over the course of 2 years in some 63 seminars, each lasting several hours (p. 58).

Thompson (1970) was both player in and conductor of a theoretical orchestra.

I found that my main job involved interpersonal relations among Indians, field workers, and staff members. . . . My most constant and difficult role turned out to be that of morale builder. . . . Someone has to keep up the morale of the group. Who is there for this job but the coordinator? I tried to handle this role as best I could in whatever way seemed appropriate: evaluating the individual's contribution to the whole, praising positive effort as well as good work, discussing problems and their possible solutions, laughing off mistakes, encouraging participation in the project at more subtle levels, placing events in a broad perspective, and especially trying to provide more personal contact and supervision. (p. 60)

HERDING CATS

Ethnographers feel both guilt and anger toward their fieldnotes—guilt because they are always behind in writing them up, and anger because they must steal so much time from observation to do so (Agar, 1996; Kleinman & Coop, 1993; Sanjek, 1990). Ethnographers begrudge time spent in writing fieldnotes; they also know it is necessary. Their obsession with writing up their notes is matched only by the satisfaction they feel when they are momentarily caught up (Kleinman & Coop, 1993, pp. 20-21).

Other tasks that take them from the "doing of fieldwork," such as staff meetings, are an altogether different story—a waste of time, perhaps, or a time to gossip with colleagues. Such attitudes, although common, also are problematic for teams, which need to meet to communicate and discuss if they are to accomplish their individual and collective tasks. Egalitarian teams, especially if "led" by reluctant or nondirective principal investigators, have difficulty taking care of common business. Or so it seemed to Stull following a site visit during the early stages of the Garden City project.

Roger Sanjek commented on how well we were doing and how impressed he was with the status of our work, the competency of each team member, and the intrateam dynamics. Personally, I feel that our team, or at least some members, may become complacent in certain areas, such as the need to be better organized, be more systematic in what we collect, and so forth. It is still my greatest frustration to try to get the members to function as a team, and not as 6 people going their separate ways. When we get together for meetings, it is virtually impossible to get them all in the same room at the same time and then keep them on track. I guess as long as we turn out a good finished product it will be okay, but I think the final product would be a lot better if people were committed to teamwork and making the most of our meetings. No one really sees these meetings as a place to do common business; no one but me tries to set and keep to common agendas. But then I think everyone looks to me to play that role. Then again, maybe I am just too anal. At one point Roger commented on how much alike he and I were, even though we come from such different traditions—compulsive, nondirectional, etc. The main difference is that he is an eternal optimist and I a devout pessimist. (Donald Stull, fieldnotes, September 13, 1988)

Stull remained nondirective and pessimistic. His notes sounded much the same the following June, when fieldwork was beginning to wind down.

I still am not moved . . . that we are a "team." While structural and logistical issues explain part of the problem, personalities, divided loyalties, . . . status jealousies and conflicts [also divide us]. (I still feel that I am treated as being higher than the rest, but also somewhat out of the loop; the others—at least Ken, Art, and Janet—have a kind of camaraderie that involves communication and discussions that I am not privy to.) Issues of Janet being the only woman, Ken the only non-Ph.D., Ken and Art's bond and sly one-upmanship in speaking Spanish around non-Spanish speakers, etc., all serve to create slight rifts.

I certainly know that I could have done a better job. I have not wanted to administer this crew, and I have felt that they have made it harder than it might have been in such things as scheduling meetings, having and sticking to agendas, etc. So I have withdrawn into myself and said the hell with it. It will get done and won't be so bad. And I have basically wanted just to do my own ethnography and be left alone. All this coupled with my lack of wanting to share anything personal with them (they know that I'm separating from my wife and carefully avoid saying anything or asking anything about my personal life—out of respect for my wishes) has made things less than perfect.

They believe, and so do I, that we have done the best job of all the teams—and I agree. Nevertheless, I wish we had done better and I think we'll begin to see the holes in the data when we start putting the book together.

Such are the dynamics of team research. As much as I hate to go back to Lawrence and end this "idyllic" period in my life, I am getting surly in my dealings with other team members, being both petrified that there is so little time left and being tired and ready to pack it in. (Donald Stull, fieldnotes, June 27, 1989)

Stull's fieldnotes reveal shortcomings common to ethnographers who find themselves leading research teams and fault lines typical of their teams. Sometimes he neglected his administrative duties for his own research, sometimes just the opposite. He expected too much of other team members—and himself. He often failed to specify what was needed and what was expected, assuming that the others shared his notions of what should get done and when. He was bothered at times by others' work habits or research styles, yet rarely did he initiate formal discussions of these matters.

Like Thompson and others before him, "interpersonal relations" took much of his time, yet some members of the team saw him as overly critical and distant. He wanted the others to follow him and complained when they did not treat him like "one of the gang." (In fact, the Garden City team called itself the "Ford Gang.") What he really wanted was to be both Roy Rogers and one of the Sons of the Pioneers.

4. THE BAGS WE PACK, THE TRIPS
WE TAKE, THE PLACES WE GO

If objectivity, rightness, and science are to be had, it is not by pretending they run free of the exertions which make or unmake them.

—Clifford Geertz (1995, p. 3)

We cannot rid ourselves of the cultural self we bring with us into the field any more than we can disown the eyes, ears, and skin through which we take in our intuitive perceptions about the new and strange world we have entered. . . . We struggle to do the best we can with the limited resources we have at hand—our ability to listen and observe carefully, empathetically, and compassionately.

—Nancy Scheper-Hughes
(1992, p. 28)

Fieldworkers are more than mere collectors of data and compilers of text. They are the objects of local gossip as well, characters who behave or misbehave according to local norms. That is, team members are expected to behave in ways that are linked to local notions of role and identity, broadly conceived to include all the aspects of the human condition that matter most.

The Zuni are said to have loved Frank Hamilton Cushing—or "Cushy," as they called him. They tried to marry him off to one of their own. They also tried him for sorcery! (Green, 1979, pp. 109-111, 157-160). Still, a half century after he left them, and almost four decades after his death in 1900, "The older people were still mourning because Cushing was not able to return from Washington" (Bertha Dutton, as quoted in Green, 1979, p. 21).

Matilda Coxe Stevenson, whose husband James led the Smithsonian's expedition to Zuni in 1879, still is remembered at Zuni as well. A Zuni woman who knew Mrs. Stevenson remembered her this way:

She was disliked by many Zunis. She lived in a camp which was guarded by two Zuni men whom she paid every day. Some of the Zunis wanted to get rid of her. You cannot believe how arrogant she was. She entered the *Kivas* [ceremonial chambers] without asking permission of the high priests. She took pictures because the Zunis did not know what she was doing. . . . But, you see, then, the Zunis were not educated and did not know what these people were doing. (quoted in Pandey, 1972, p. 326)

They certainly do now. Triloki Pandey could name two score ethnographers who worked at Zuni in the century after Cushing and Mrs. Stevenson blazed the trail for them. Part of their legacy has been a community increasingly resistant to researchers. In 1941, for example, the Zuni tribal council confiscated an anthropologist's fieldnotes, burned part of them, and expelled him from the pueblo (Pandey, 1972, p. 322). Lurie (1966, p. 55) believes Mrs. Stevenson must shoulder some of the blame. But Pandey (1972) finds the blame—or credit—in all of us—in the "sex and personality differences of the observers, level of their involvement in the life of the people studied, their values and personal preferences, the research tasks they set up for themselves, and the roles they adopt" (p. 335).

Gender and ethnicity are only two of the possible slates onto which research teams and their members' identities are written by the local community. In team research, different genders, ages, ethnicities, and backgrounds simultaneously intrude on and enable the team's efforts to "listen and observe carefully."

It is difficult enough for solo ethnographers to manage their roles in the field. Norris Brock Johnson, an African American, felt excluded from the white tourist (and tourist service) community in the Windward Islands (Johnson, 1984). At the same time, local boat builders were, for a time, unwilling to admit him as a participant in their ranked, high-status, masculine world. They wrote him off as a suspicious character, possibly a black revolutionary from neighboring Granada.

Likewise, when Garden City locals learned that Jose Cintron, the Garden City project's original school ethnographer, was uncomfortable amid pickup trucks, cornfields, and feedyards, he was branded a "city boy," and the talk—sometimes conspiratorially and not too helpfully shared by other team members—turned to Cintron's difficulties in adjusting to Garden City.

The move from uncomfortable, misfit, or culture-shocked outsider to (grudgingly) accepted semimember has to be bridged by individual ethnographers. But team attention to the process of community ascription of role, and ethnographic negotiations about it, can smooth the pathways to rapport and acceptance among host communities and team members. Johnson (1984) found that acceptance into the company of both midwestern women teachers and island craftsmen was a process with predictable stages—ritual steps of exclusion, testing, and demonstration of the fieldworker's native-like skill. Rapport depended on willingness to learn and perform in ways that signaled the ethnographer's respect of insider perspectives on the world. When it works, the respect can become mutual, and the ethnographer may find himself or herself amid new collaborators.

Johnson (1984) reminds fieldworkers that they will have to stop, wait, and cross boundaries, seen and unseen, if they hope to enter another social system. Each step is a substage within the second or transitional stage of Van Gennep's (1960) tripartite model of human rites of passage. These steps along the way to provisional group acceptance are, of course, filtered through local meanings, local talk, and local understandings about gender, ethnicity, status, and identity.

Many a novice fieldworker stumbles along the way to establishing rapport (Hill, 1974); some fall. Some get up, dust themselves off, and keep on going; some turn aside. Cintron was a Puerto Rican from Chicago. He did not like Garden City, and he did not like the racial discourse that was part of the way in which the community accommodated its newcomers. Nor did he fit into local categories of ethnicity, where Latinos were classified as either "Mexicans" or "wetbacks," no matter their national origin or legal status (Stull, 1990a, p. 311). We really could not fault Cintron when he left the team 6 months into the project for a tenure-track position at a university on the West Coast. No one will blame Johnson, either, for not building a field bridge into the perceptions of racist white tourists on his Caribbean island. But the knowledge Johnson and Cintron could have gained and shared with the rest of us dies aborning when the solo researcher, permanently stopped while in transition, moves on to other things.

Teams, in an ideal setting where professional egos are trimmed and assuaged, might allow such turning away by following up with a turning toward by other team members, other not quite blank slates on which the community can write a more workable field identity. Teams can experiment, sending others to the arenas in which one team member or another is unable or unwilling to embrace a workable role.

Negotiating a field role already is a difficult task without team members having to manage their roles in relation to the other members of the field team. So, there is a danger that teams will spend so much time dealing with their individual and team identities that they will neglect the work of getting to know their field site. In light of this, teams are not necessarily more efficient than lone rangers in getting their work done, but they can be much more productive when the rites of passage are through.

Although all potential categories of individual difference are culture-bound constructions, they are nonetheless part of the lived experience of ethnographic research teams. Team members, like lone ranger ethnographers, have to step across boundaries and pass through the rites of fieldwork and teamwork without creating too much interpersonal or psychic havoc. This is easier said than done. Like many of their successors to team ethnography, Cushing and Mrs. Stevenson had little use for one another. He complained of her methods and of "the envy, not to say jealousy, of others in our party (especially of the *lady* member who has constituted such a leading spirit in it)"; she thought Cushing was "the biggest fool and charlatan I ever knew" (quoted in Green, 1990, pp. 43, 351). Despite all the insults they hurled at one another, both were ethnographic pioneers. Cushing has enjoyed renewed recognition in recent years; Mrs. Stevenson is all but forgotten (Parezo, 1993c).

Team Togetherness: (We're)
Looking Better Every Beer

There are two kinds of togetherness in team research: togetherness in building the team and togetherness in the doing of fieldwork. Both can be problematic. Don Stull's notes from the early days of the Garden City project brim with the mention of team togetherness, usually over food and often, like our first all-team get-together, over drinks as well. Being together is important for new teams because it is an outward and visible enactment of the individual's transition into membership. Subsequent projects by members of the Changing Relations Project (Erickson, Grey, & Stull, 1990; Stull, Erickson, & Giner, 1996) took shape without these lengthy team-building warm-ups. We already had stopped, waited, then entered acceptable team roles. But new teams have to ease their adjustment to the new community and to one another at the same time. This has to happen while the local community is holding the newcomer researchers at arm's length, at the stopping stage. So, team members spend too much time together, avoiding the sting of nonmembership, the loneliness of being a stranger in a strange place.

A loner talks more to group members; as part of an ethnographic team, one probably tends to seek other members of the team for company. That is a tendency that team members must be concerned with. (Agar, 1996, p. 250)

Togetherness by team members has implications both for team building and for the quality of the ethnographic research product. Team togetherness over food and drink raises particularly interesting issues. Food and alcohol lend structure to social life, and they often do so in ways that highlight differences in status and role (Douglas, 1987). So, although alcohol is a kind of social lubricant, it may lead to unintended consequences through differential participation by team members or through the local shape and texture ascribed to team members' participation. The team must attend not only to individual social norms but also to norms governing group behavior, and it may not be locally approved for mixed-age or mixed-gender groups to unwind (or wind up) in this way.

Regardless of the local community's view of the team, it is a fact that information shared over the second beer often is of a different character than information shared over the first. So, team members who, out of sensitivity to local norms or personal inclination, are not a part of moderate feasting and team-based imbibing miss out on more than the integrative aspects of these team rites of passage. Excluded members will be unable to share the gossip the next morning; they miss the empirical content of experiential tellings and retellings. Care has to be taken to ensure that all team members get the same sense of belonging and the same opportunities to learn what their teammates are learning, regardless of their personally or culturally constructed level of participation in shared ritual time. Fieldworkers need not be good-time charlies, but they must be aware of the social functions of food and drink in team building and take the implications of differential participation seriously. This is especially the case for new teams.

Seeing the same thing at the same time, but differently, is something that only team researchers can do. But, as Rivers noted, the "excitement" of more than one ethnographer per setting can become a nuisance (quoted in Stocking, 1983, p. 92). Here lies the problem of too much togetherness while doing research, as we found out when we decided to record a bull session we were having with one of our key informants and a reporter from *Life*, who was in town to do a story based on our research.

> The conversation was very interesting between Bill [the reporter] and Tulio [our friend and key informant], with the rest of us chipping in and discussing things that we often do not get a chance to talk about. Debriefing ourselves in the kind of brainstorming session that can be very productive—partly this was that Bill was asking questions that we had not thought to ask or questions in ways and of people that we had not done. I decided this is crazy not to record

this, so I went to the bedroom and got my [recorder], came into the living room, plugged it in the socket by Tulio, and began setting it up. Bill asked what I was doing and I told him. He looked at me funny but kept on going. Art and Jose also started taping, then hooked up their super-duper mike to my machine. We all went about our normal conversations in what I thought was a natural and very productive manner.

After about 30 minutes, Bill said to me, "This tape recorder is really bothering me." We were talking about IBP [formerly Iowa Beef Packers], and he had been making some evil capitalist-type statements. I said, "We'll turn it off, then." I'm not sure what his problem [was]. He said something about how he wanted assurances that his comments wouldn't appear in any of our reports. What followed was an interchange, a monologue mainly, in which I explained quickly informed consent and the anthropologist's approach to protecting informants. He said okay, but I think [he] was still perturbed about it. I think part of his problem was the fact that all of a sudden he was our subject; "the worm had turned." (Donald Stull, fieldnotes, July 3, 1988)

The situation really did not require more than one ethnographer, and when the scene moved from participatory conversation to recorded interview, the meaning of the interaction changed. The worm that had turned was an intersubjective one, turning away from participation and creating distance. The team stopped being conversation partners and started being inquisitors. Too many researchers at a time may spoil the soup, and cooks are not the same thing as friends. It takes friends—or some similarly safe, trusting, and accessible local role—to make relatively free-range conversation possible. Earlier in the day, however, when Art, Jose, and Don were getting acquainted with Bill over breakfast, he had been the inquisitor: "While he mixed the conversation with polite chitchat about backgrounds, sports, and so forth, he never moves very far from the business at hand. His reporter's pad comes out at the drop of a hat" (Donald Stull, fieldnotes, July 3, 1988).

Annie Gets Her Guns

Gender—community expectations about it and research team presentation of it—marks just one of the border zones that fieldworkers encounter, although arguably one of the most important. Although gender expectations seem to be broached by human behavior more often than they contain and restrict it, these expectations are important nevertheless. The CRP-Garden City team's only female member, Janet Benson, moderated our five men's potential for gender myopia, just as we and the CRP national board had hoped. Teams without gender diversity may miss and misinterpret a great deal in their fieldwork.

> I was the only woman on the research team, and the only individual with child-care responsibilities. It was easier for me to interact informally with women than with men, which biased me originally toward the study of families rather than single males; on the other hand, male researchers could socialize more freely with male workers and tended to adopt male perspectives. We disagreed for some time on how to characterize packinghouse work in reference to gender. While the male researchers tended to discuss it as a single-male occupation, I was struck by the almost universal participation of Laotian and Vietnamese women in packinghouse employment. (Benson, 1994, p. 101)

Without gender diversity, field researchers may miss many of the available interpretations and issues lived by community members. This is true in a much wider sense than suggested by Griaul (1957, p. 15), who saw mixed-gender research teams as important to access social settings from which one or the other gender was excluded. CRP monitors, sent out from the project board, provided frequent reminders to pay attention to gender issues of all kinds and to be in the right places to understand gender-related things. One monitor wrote, "Often got sense that discussion with team members focused on male perspectives. Be sure female positions are also covered" (Karen Ito, memorandum to CRP board and Garden City team, June 6, 1989).

To respond to this concern, shared by everyone on the team, our research had to ensure that male and female fields of experience came within reach of our eyes, ears, and notebooks. That was easy enough; both men and the woman on our team were able, after a while, to hear from both men and women. We struggled, however, with overidentifying with our closest informants (who, ironically, often proved to be members of the opposite sex), their experiences, and their interpretations. Team members are, in most field settings, likely to be in the right place at the right time to learn about local constructions and contests about gender and gender relations. The challenge for teams is to generate those opportunities and situate the analysis within the researchers' experience and understanding. Here again, team diversity in access to roles and settings helps.

For example, the historical circumstances surrounding Southeast Asian immigration to Garden City, and the ebb and flow of changing gender relations among Southeast Asian families, provided the team with opportunities to see ideas about men and women as they were discussed, lived out, and contested. In Garden City, these events sometimes took place without much regard for the ethnographer's gender. The ethnographer just happened to be in the right place at the right time. Propinquity matters, and propinquity depends on the host community's willingness to grant the fieldworker passage from the stopping stage to some form of participation. Paying attention to gender issues in this way sometimes becomes an individual project. Teams can take advantage of the lone ethnographer's solitary field role, sending members out to collect and interpret events alone. Ken Erickson, whose commitment to the project was limited (on paper at least) to 10% of his time as a refugee social service administrator, was in the right place to provide access to agency files that reflected the local history of institutional accommodation among newcomers and established residents. He had access to gatherings of social service staff, where gender and ethnicity were used to act out individual accommodation to an evolving set of new-immigrant experiences.

One evening, Erickson and 15 refugee social service workers were gathered at a Colorado resort for a regional conference and training session. They talked and joked after an improvised Vietnamese supper. A Vietnamese woman, Muoi, the director of a social service program in another state, posed the following question to the group during a lull in the conversation: "You know, God did create man first—and then woman. But do you know how woman got her name, 'Woman'?" Van, one of the Garden City case workers, said something about woman being created from man's ribs, and then he asked Muoi, playfully, if she wanted to count his ribs by way of verification. Muoi, ignoring him, went on: "Man at that time did not have much language. Just living alone there, he didn't know the name for woman, so when God put him to sleep, and then he woke up and woman was there, the man looked at her, and he said, like this, 'Whooah! Man!' And that's how woman got her name." When the laughter died down, another man said, "Well, look, you women were so nice and traditional. You cooked this fine Vietnamese meal for all us men!" "Oh," said Kim, one of the cooks, a friend of Muoi. "That is where you are wrong. You see, we cooked for ourselves, and we already ate first, and we are so kind that we just gave you the leftovers!" (Ken Erickson, fieldnotes, January 27, 1988).

This exchange was not orchestrated by our team. Our structured interviews on male-female relations usually elicited prefabricated restatements of Vietnamese women's supportive roles. Women, despite their presence on the floors of the packing plants, often were portrayed as managing the kitchen and staying outside the so-called mainstream of political and community life. This "traditional" set of household gender expectations was even reenacted for one of the scenes in the project video, *America Becoming* (Kim-Gibson, 1990), in which a Vietnamese woman is shown serving food to a group of men meeting in a trailer house to make funeral arrangements for a departed kinsman. The woman was shown looking on, silent, from the kitchen. This was not a film editor's choice but rather was the role she and her kinsmen acted out in a self-conscious reconstruction for the camera crew.

The version of gender relations this women and her family recreated for public display was a far cry from the good-natured bantering between the Vietnamese social service workers over dinner. By tapping different arenas—home reenactment for public consumption, formal interviews, and participation in institutional settings—the team witnessed a broad enough range of attitudes and behaviors to be wary of simplistic statements about gender relations in Garden City.

Our team was not representative of the community's ethnic and gender makeup. Had we been blessed with more eyes to see and more ears to hear, Garden City's story might be better told. But we tried to understand and we tried to encourage one another to travel the pathway of fieldwork, a road built by many unseen hands. Teams, no less than the refugee social service workers, need settings that help them learn to travel together.

The Vietnamese dinner provides a useful model for team building. It engaged participants in making explicit the ongoing contest over authority, place, and recognition among men and women refugees. It was acted out in jokes and play after—and only after—the sharing of food and drink. It took place on neutral ground, in a kind of liminal space, after a meal cooked by no particular family during training explicitly designed to bring subsurface tensions into the open. It allowed newcomer social service workers to search for ways in which to cope with the serious community and family dysfunctions that arose in Garden City, a place where newcomers and established residents often resisted mainstream American definitions and understandings about community and family "problems." These social service workers, like other newcomers (including our team), were recasting their own roles—making new rules. All this was followed by work, training, and learning in tightly focused training sessions. Ethnographic teams can take a lesson from these Vietnamese social service workers about the need to create opportunities for team building, balanced by time for working and learning.

Ethnographic teams function best when safe space for exploring dimensions of difference and strategies for boundary crossing is present. This means building two-way trust—among the team and between team members and their informants in the field. It also means finding a balance among teamwork, team building, and the learning that must get done by team members together and alone.

Creating that safe space can have a downside, of course, and cultural conventions for safe space are different for male and female ethnographers (and their hosts) in different cultural settings (Lee, 1995). Ethnography, as a job, can too easily take on the same segregated, compartmentalized scheme of work organization that characterizes the modern factory (Knokke, 1994). Teams beware. Catharsis on the couch or at the bar must be followed by a return to the less open, more structured world of work. Ethnographic teams have to select the structures into which they wish to mold their "teamness."

Too often, perhaps, the CRP-Garden City ethnographers took a rather stereotypical path—men to the bar and the packing plant, women to the household. But that was only part of the story. The reality was more complex. Although the public school, in the United States at least, is generally a place where women work and men oversee (Grogan, 1996; Johnson, 1984), our team's male school ethnographers, Jose Cintron and Mark Grey, found their way. Janet Benson was able to interview men whom Stull, despite his best efforts, could never coax to the tape recorder but Stull's best friends in Garden City turned out to be women. So, the actual work of bridging the gap between the team and the community is essentially an individual project after all, but one that the team as a group can limit, direct, and facilitate.

Each member of an ethnographic research team must both discover and test the historically constructed tensions, attractions, and distractions that tug individually at them. Simply put, the ethnicity of the fieldworker and the diversity within the team are not sufficient to guarantee easy access to the company of strangers. They are sometimes necessary but never sufficient. Still, gender and ethnicity are among the dimensions of difference that ethnographers can employ to their advantage.

5. PACKING IT IN, WRITING IT UP,
AND GETTING IT OUT THE DOOR

I am more convinced than ever that the way to do field work is just never to come up for air until it is all over.

—Margaret Mead (1970, p. 310)

Each piece of knowledge that either member of the team acquires speeds up the learning of the other or others. If this is accepted enthusiastically, without rivalry, then any team of whatever composition, but especially one contrasted in sex or age, will be able to do, not twice, but four or five times as much work as one person working alone. However, differential self-esteem and competitiveness are very likely to accompany any field work.

—Margaret Mead (1970, p. 326)

Data are not properly "sociology" until they are published. If unpublished, knowledge perishes.

—Gary Alan Fine (1993, p. 270)

John Van Maanen (1995b) tells us that ethnography consists of "three rather distinct activity phases or moments" (p. 5). The first is fieldwork. But its seconds tick away all too soon. Whether we are ready or not, time, money, energy, and tolerance run out, usually at about the same time. The second moment commences when the ethnographer(s) begin(s) writing up the study's results.[3] This can be as demanding as fieldwork, often more so for teams. Mead (1970) knew what she was talking about when she said, "Field work is individualistic; ideally each young anthropologist wants to write a whole book about a whole culture" (p. 326).

Most of what is written and said about ethnography concerns its first moment—fieldwork (Van Maanen, 1995a, p. 5). Only in the last decade has writing, ethnography's second moment, received much attention (Clifford & Marcus, 1986; Geertz, 1988; Richardson, 1990; Van Maanen, 1988; Wolf, 1992). Some would say we have turned our backs on fieldwork in a belated attempt to give ethnographies their due. It seems that way at times.

But most ethnographers probably still spend far more time considering the ways of fieldwork than the ways of reporting it. In any event, "how one moves from a period of lengthy field study to a written account based on such study is by no means obvious" (Van Maanen, 1995a, p. 6). If this is true for ethnography in general, it is twice true for team ethnography. Words such as "polyphony" and "polyvocality" are much in vogue these days. They most certainly describe both the processes and products of team research. But those who throw these terms around mean something else by them. They use them to refer to the dialogue between the observer and the observed, to the recasting of the ethnographer's power in ways that give informants greater voice and authority and that democratize authorial responsibility or at least give it a more democratic veneer (Clifford, 1986, p. 15; Tyler, 1986, p. 127). But transforming the different voices of a team's members, not to mention those of their hosts, into a polyphonic fugue, much less a symphony, is quite something else again.

Despite the recent "realization that anthropologists produce not truth but texts" (Moore, 1994, p. 345), no one is saying too much about the production line itself. Oh, now that Sanjek (1990) finally broke the code of silence on fieldnotes, we are beginning to write about how to make useful notes (Emerson, Fretz, & Shaw, 1995). And Becker (1986) has written the essential writing guide for social scientists. But how are teams to transform their many voices into one? Or should they?

Margaret Gibson and her project codirector submitted separate reports at the close of the Punjabi Education Project (Gibson, 1987). W. Lloyd Warner directed the analysis of the Yankee City findings and wrote, or served as senior coauthor on, all the volumes that came out of the study (Sanjek, 1990, p. 330). And Clyde Kluckhohn combined his notes with those of colleagues for *Navaho Witchcraft* (1944).

There is no one right way for teams to write up their product; the right way is the one that works the best. And the best way is the one that transforms data into an acceptable narrative most efficiently. "Getting it out the door" is the order of the day in meatpacking (Stull, Broadway, & Erickson, 1992). It is the same in social science: "Your research project isn't done until you have written it up and launched it into the conversation by publishing it" (Becker, 1986, p. 124).

Meatpacking and team research are much alike. Each is a bloody business. In one, workers transform a live animal into a carcass and then break it down into cuts of meat that find their way to the grocer's meat counter, ultimately to end up on someone's dinner plate, only to be cut up once again, chewed, swallowed, and digested. In the other, workers extract information from live animals and then transform it into words and numbers, which are in turn built into new narratives. These are further processed (to borrow yet another term from the food industry) into texts, which are then published (hopefully) for consumption (Van Maanen's third ethnographic moment) by professional colleagues and others. They, too, chew our words. We want readers to swallow, digest, and be nourished by them. But there are times when they spit them out, only to chew us up instead.

> My last two weeks in the field were hectic and not nearly as productive as I would have liked. Much of my time was spent in writing a . . . grant [proposal] to get money for a photo exhibit at the [Finney County] Historical Society (and to supplement our trip back in November to do public forums [on our findings]). [The museum's director] did a little of the writing, but I did the bulk. I also had to write my part of the preliminary report on . . . power relations, edit everybody else's into a coherent whole, and get it off in the mail. (Donald Stull, fieldnotes, August 9-24, 1989)

From early in our formal education until relatively late, we are instructed in the art of writing—how to spell, what to capitalize, where to put commas and periods. Whether by formal instruction, friendly advice, imitation, osmosis, or the stinging critiques of editors, we learn to write according to professional expectations. Such instruction is not always a blessing, but at least someone is pointing the way (Becker, 1986).

All of this instruction, formal as well as informal, assumes that we are writing up our own material by ourselves. Nobody tells us how to write with others. Becker (1986) devotes only six paragraphs to coauthorship, recounting an attempt to get his students to write a paper together when he had run out of "entertainments to fill the remaining seminar hours" (p. 23). The joint writing project died aborning amid squabbles over whose names should appear where and lack of follow-through after the class ended. In the end, "if the work is to be done at all (and usually it isn't), one of the survivors must take it on as an individual project" (p. 25). Becker did, and the result was the opening chapter of *Writing for Social Scientists*.

Postmodernism has been much concerned with ethnographic writing, both the "reality they represent and the authoritative selves of . . . authors," maintaining that "claims to empirical accuracy cannot be true universally since description itself is an author's construction" (Downey & Rogers, 1995, p. 270). The omniscient and invisible ethnographer has been supplanted by the self-reflexive purveyor of "partial truths" (Clifford, 1986).

The pluralistic stance of postmodernists, and their concern with ethnographic voice, ought to lead them to a discussion of professional collaboration and coauthorship. It has not. There is concern, most certainly, with theoretical positions, and there is much posturing to go with it. Authors call for more conversation and less polemic if we are to fruitfully exchange ideas. Downey and Rogers (1995) even trumpet a new strategy of "partnering":

> It envisions acts of academic theorizing as undertaken in partner relations with their interlocutors in collective, but temporary, negotiations of knowledge production. We are thinking of partnering not as a market activity, a business partnership, but as a variety of activities of exchange among committed cohabitants. (p. 273)

Sounds great, but team research and the messy business of reaching common understanding are not what they mean.

> We headed out to Oakley for our team retreat on Sunday afternoon. [We chose this small town on the High Plains of northwest Kansas because it was equally out of the way for us all. We hoped a couple of days holed up together on neutral ground—away from the demands of our individual professional and personal lives—would enable us to come up with a prospectus for our ethnography on Garden City.] As usual, in spite of our best intentions, something got in the way of our efforts—in this case, having to go back [to Garden City] for the Board of Education meeting on Monday night.
>
> Monday was one long and very frustrating meeting of our team in Oakley, in which we spent the morning trying to get a handle on the book outline and the afternoon coming to the conclusion that some of us . . . could not or would not make the kind of commitment necessary to complete a book (there was also the recurrent problem of trying to get closure on what the book would be like and what its theme would be—every time we seemed to be getting agreement on something, it would slip away). . . . Michael was especially frustrated with the rest of the team. . . . It was finally he who forced everybody's hand by coming into the afternoon meeting saying he was pulling out and would not participate in the writing of the book. This was like a bombshell, because his work is viewed as central to the book, he is one of the best liked of all the members (though he doesn't necessarily reciprocate those feelings to everyone), and, finally, there is this strong but unwritten agreement that we will all go forward to do the book—this is especially important to Janet.
>
> As a result of Michael's statement—something to the effect that he was willing to commit his time and money to seeing this thing through—we all went around the room discussing what we could and couldn't do. I made it

clear that we would need several face-to-face meetings where we hammered out differences and critiqued each other's work and that we would have to set reasonable deadlines and meet them. I came down pretty hard on several people about not meeting deadlines and about not pulling their weight. I was the only one who really said what he felt, though others made stabs at it (Art: "I don't want to have this book be just another bunch of whites doing an ethnography").

The meeting disintegrated that afternoon, and we agreed to all give some serious thought to the project and come back the next morning to decide what we were to do. Ken, Mark, and I went off to [Garden City, and] the others stayed behind. The next morning, things were pretty much the same, no one had anything new to say. Janet did not want to surrender the idea of the book and insisted on writing the prospectus. . . . Ken made perhaps the best statement, that we should see if we could get our act together to do the *Urban Anthropology* collection and then take it from there. We did, but the quality is uneven [see Stull, 1990b].

When we broke up on Tuesday after lunch, there seemed to be unspoken relief on the part of some, maybe all, that we no longer had THE BOOK hanging over our head, though Janet continued to cling to it, unwilling to admit defeat. On our trip up to Lexington [Nebraska], Michael expressed remorse and guilt for throwing a monkey wrench in the works, but I assured him, honestly, that he did the right thing—forcing each of us to face the reality of what we could do and what we were willing to commit to—Mark off to a new job at [Northern Iowa University], Art taking on more administration while Caroline [his new wife] places considerable demands on his personal time (and resents his work in GC), Ken with the ever-present demands of SRS [Kansas Department of Social and Rehabilitation Services] and his tendency to flit from one thing to another, Michael and I embarking on the Lexington project [see Broadway, 1991; Gouveia & Stull, 1995], and several of us with extensive writing commitments. (Donald Stull, fieldnotes, May 21, 1990)

Louise Lamphere, codirector of the Changing Relations Project (CRP), edited two volumes of ethnographic essays drawn from the national study. One consists of a chapter from each of the six sites on what she considered its strongest material (Lamphere, 1992); the other, *Newcomers in the Workplace* (Lamphere, Stepick, & Grenier, 1994), contains several chapters each on Garden City, Miami, and Philadelphia. Lamphere also negotiated an agreement with Temple University Press to publish an ethnography from each site. Benson and Stull prepared a prospectus with the rest of the team's permission. They would write the book, drawing on everyone's materials, and would circulate the manuscript for everyone's input. The book has yet to be written.

Riesman and Watson (1964) could have been speaking for the Garden City team when they explained why they did not produce a monograph.

> The dispersion of project staff members and the accompanying commitment to new projects and obligations tells part of the story of why the Sociability Project is still unfinished. It is not the whole story. . . . Differences in emphasis and point of view which had been glossed over during the period of data collection returned to haunt us as we tried to prepare written reports of our accomplishments. (p. 310)

Of the six teams that made up the CRP, two have published full-length ethnographies—Philadelphia (Goode & Schneider, 1994) and Monterey Park (Horton, 1995). Why only two? Team organization plays a part. Pyramidal teams, with a project director at the top who oversees and directs other members' activity, are more likely to produce full-length ethnographies. In such projects, the principal investigator will find it relatively easy to mold the data collected by the rest of the team, often graduate students, into an integrated, coherent narrative. The author's interpretation of the data becomes the team's interpretation; her or his voice is the one through which we hear the team. This is top-down writing. Like top-down planning, it may not provide the best representation of the people's (or team's) ideas, but it is the most efficient way to "get it out the door."

Those CRP teams composed mainly of professional peers and organized in flat social structures have not pulled their findings into books. That is not to say that they have been less productive than those that have. But for the Garden City team, and we suspect for others, polyvocality is a mixed blessing. We have each presented our "partial truths," sometimes with other team members and sometimes alone. But aside from our project report (Stull et al., 1990), we have not spoken with one voice.

Riesman and Watson (1964) offer another part of the answer. When the Garden City team met in Oakley in May 1990, we already were scattered from Colorado to New York. We still are. We also had basic disagreements about what we had found, what it meant, and how we should present it. We still do.

Polyvocality is a watchword of postmodernism. But "a team that speaks with more than one voice is doomed" (Gow, 1991, p. 12). Agencies are not interested in polyvocality; ask Gibson (1987). Book publishers are not much different. Most are not interested in edited volumes, and even fewer want ethnographies that look like them. So, research teams must reach some form of consensus. "The team leader certainly does not have carte blanche to lobby for his own personal prejudices, biases, and unfounded opinions. On the contrary, he or she should lobby for those ideas agreed upon through consensus with the team" (Gow, 1991, p. 12). The Garden City team tried to do just that, but when it came time to draft the final report (or the interim report, for that matter), we found ourselves scattered across half a continent. Like most people who write with others, we divided up the work. The final report had to answer five questions—questions that had guided the CRP from the beginning (Bach, 1993, p. 18).

One question, about the impact of macrolevel socioeconomic processes on relations between new immigrants and established residents, clearly belonged to Broadway, our geographer and token quantitative researcher. We merrily left it to him (see Broadway, 1990). The other four questions required input from the rest of us. What is the nature of relations among established residents and new immigrants? What are the conceptions of American identity and American life, and how do these shape intergroup interactions? What are the power relations among new immigrants and established residents? What situations and strategies promote communication, accommodation, and accord in situations where there are multigroup interactions?

Team members wrote answers to each question for "their people" and "their arenas" of activity (workplaces, schools, social service agencies, etc.). They relied on their fieldnotes and transcriptions of almost 300 tape-recorded interviews to provide ethnographic data and vignettes (Stull et al., 1990, pp. 15-25). Each team member sent paper and electronic copies of his or her write-ups to Stull, who combined, edited, and in some cases rewrote them for interim and final reports. He often dipped into his own fieldnotes and interviews to expand and embellish others' sections. Each draft was then sent back out to the team for comments, suggestions, and revisions; however, final decisions on content, interpretation, arrangement, and style rested with Stull. Members also submitted policy recommendations, which were reviewed, discussed, and modified as needed by the entire team.

No one was completely satisfied with the final report. Certain members were uncomfortable with Stull's folksy writing style, influenced by Mike Agar and *Tales of the Field* (Van Maanen, 1988), which he read early in this fieldwork. Others took exception to certain interpretations and recommendations. One felt that the final report shortchanged the literature on ethnicity, so we compromised and let that person put such a discussion in an appendix. The closing lines of our report sum it up as well as any:

> We continue to differ on the nature and extent of change [in relations between new immigrants and established residents in Garden City]. Our disagreements reflect, in microcosm, different perspectives on the nature of American society—among social scientists and among the different ethnic groups in Garden City and beyond. (Stull et al., 1990, p. 129)

Neither were all of the report's audiences overjoyed with it. Some on the CRP national board did not approve of our plans for disseminating the report to Garden City. Our conclusions and recommendations did not please some established residents in Garden City. But in the end, both audiences accepted and benefited from the report. The Ford Foundation later funded members of our team to do research in another beefpacking town (Lexington, Nebraska) and hold a national conference on meat processing's impact on host communities (Stull, Broadway, & Griffith, 1995). The school district, social service providers, and government of Garden City have implemented some of our recommendations and used our publications in grant and contract proposals.

Moving On

Teams must be built; they also must be dismantled. For some, this is no problem. Hired guns partner up for a brief time and a specific task; then they move on to the next job with a new gang (Gow, 1991). Sometimes members, soured on personal and professional differences, want to put as much daylight as they can between themselves and their teammates.

But for many research teams, breaking up is hard—sometimes harder than the initial courtship or even the union itself. After working—and living—together for such a long time, members may find professional life apart from the team hard to imagine. Deep personal bonds of lasting friendship and commitment form.

> Concentrating together on a challenging real problem over a period of months and even years, we formed close friendships that encompassed an unusual bond. It was the comradeship that comes from worrying and laughing together, from working through psychological problems, and from defending our joint findings when they were questioned or attacked. It is the "togetherness" of a common endeavor, as when Alice Joseph and I worked out, day by day and

point by point on the basis of project findings, the integration of Hopi personality with Hopi culture, mythology, art, ceremonial, and worldview in the context of the ecology and history. We often experienced the thrill of mutual recognition when suddenly a long-sought resolution to a problem flashed into consciousness. So *The Hopi Way* (Thompson & Joseph, 1944/1967) was forged. We had to buck many popular stereotypes regarding the Hopi tribe, as inevitably happens in multidisciplinary research.

The loneliness of the anthropologist working single-handed on a remote South Sea island is absent in team research. . . . In times of discouragement as well as elation, I looked to my friends and coworkers for understanding and support. (Thompson, 1970, pp. 60-61)

As the project winds down, some members realize they are not cut out for team research and take their leave, remaining friends but going their own ways. Others find that they just plain like one another and like working together, so they search for ways to continue personal and professional partnerships. It is in this way that teams reinvent themselves.

So it was with the CRP-Garden City team. Erickson, Grey, and Stull (1990) took time from the Oakley conference to deliver their report to the Garden City School Board on a study they had been commissioned to do on teacher turnover. Broadway and Stull left that same meeting the next day to begin fieldwork in Lexington, where they conducted research on and off for several years. They continue to work and write together. In 1994, Erickson and Stull joined with Miguel Giner, a colleague of Erickson's, to study the corporate and work culture of a packing plant in another town (Stull, Erickson, and Giner, 1996).

Several of us have very similar professional interests, we like working together, and we know what each does best and what to expect of one another. And we have added new partners to our band, not just social scientists but also service providers and other professionals from Garden City and the other communities in which we have worked. So, whenever new projects present themselves, the initial contact person calls those he or she feels are best suited for the job. It is a geographically dispersed, ever changing, but tightly knit and deeply committed confederation of re-searchers—musketeers who know they can count on one another to do the job, do it right, and do it on time. Such is the makeup of successful long-term research collaboration.

6. TO TEAM OR NOT TO TEAM?

Researchers are lone rangers, cowboys, individualists. Analysis is private, fieldnotes are rarely available for secondary analysis, and much ethnographic writing is accepted on faith.

—Gary Alan Fine (1993, p. 269)

In the old model of ethnography, an ethnographer worked alone. He or she went off and spent a great deal of time with a small group of people. Then he or she returned and—still alone—crafted an image of that small group. Where was the quality control, I wondered?

—Michael H. Agar (1996, p. 14)

Tonto is dead. The Lone Ranger now sits in the bunkhouse in a self-reflexive mood (Hackenberg, 1993, 1994; Moore, 1994). What is he to do? Should he hang up his spurs and gun belt, cash in his silver bullets, and retire to the veranda, there to rock his days away pondering the others in them tha'r hills and his role in shaping anthropological tall tales about them? No, he has trails left to ride and knots left to tie, and out by the corral Roy, Dale, and all those sonsofpioneers are singing "Happy Trails." Maybe he will just buckle on his résumé, mosey on over, and see whether they could use another top hand.

But is partnering up all that easy—for the Masked Man or for ethnography? No, it ain't. Besides, there are good reasons for riding alone—logistical, methodological, professional, perhaps even cultural ones.

Our perspective on team ethnography is an American one. In fact, it is a perspective shaped largely by the experiences of American ethnographers studying other Americans. American ethnographers, whether working at home or working abroad, seem to have many of the same experiences, but what of ethnographers from other national and academic traditions? According to Tedlock (1991, p. 69), the ethnographic tradition that emerged in France during the early 20th century emphasized team research and documentary sources, whereas the British and American traditions emphasized individual research and participant observation.

The French fieldwork tradition was initiated during the 1920s by Marcel Mauss and Maurice Delafosse, who, together with Levy-Bruhl and River, founded

53

the Institut d'Ethnologie. . . . Marcel Mauss, although he never undertook fieldwork, . . . recommended that the "professional ethnographer" adopt the "intensive method" by which he did not mean long-term individual experiential research, but rather multifaceted documentary team research, resulting in hundreds of sound recordings, textual accounts, and major collections of art and artifacts. (p. 83)

Although we do not agree with Tedlock (1991) on the role of team ethnography in the American (and British) tradition, her points are well taken. Are teams more prevalent and more accepted in the ethnographic traditions of our colleagues trained and working in Latin America, in Eastern Europe, or in the Far East? Do their teams look like ours, do they function in much the same manner, and do they run up against the same problems? We really cannot say. We put aside the discussion of married teams in Chapter 1; we do the same here for team ethnography in other national traditions. Both are important discussions, and both we leave for another time.

There is more to how research gets done than just national style; there is the culture of the academy itself. In Chapter 3, we argued that the cult of individualism is the state religion of academia. The religion of academic individualism is expressed in custom and is rooted in structure. In reviewing an early draft of this manuscript, John Van Maanen pointed out the following:

> Despite all logic, one can only get a Ph.D. by a single-authored dissertation (even though we know fully well that even dissertations are collective endeavors). . . . Tenure comes largely through single-authored papers or monographs, not joint ones. Encouraging team ethnography in this context has its career dangers, and they are often formidable. (personal communication, January 3, 1997)

True enough, and certainly truer for ethnographers than for our more quantitative or experimental colleagues. Still, joint authorship always has been an accepted practice in social science, if not necessarily the norm; and, besides, individual team members regularly write up "their own" material.

The cult of individualism reveals itself in more than our solitary pilgrimages to the shrines of publication. It is, to borrow a title from one who walked the earth in ethnography's heroic age, *la vida*. And *the life* must be lived "without other white men, right among the natives." It must be so, for it was foretold to us by Malinowski when he came back from Omarakana. Like Moses when he came down from Sinai, Malinowski had good reason for his commandments. "Anthropologists undergo self-expansion and enlarge their range of perceptions and sensitivities when they do fieldwork. The changes in personal values, self-feelings and attitudes toward others are often profound" (Spindler, 1970, p. v). These changes are what make anthropologists, and anthropologists are a different breed than other social scientists, even those who practice the craft of ethnography (Agar, 1996, pp. 39-40).

What Berreman (1962) called the human experience of fieldwork is pivotal in defining ethnography and socializing its members, at least the anthropological ones. And we should not forget how important lone ranger ethnography has been in developing the image of "anthropologist as hero" (Sontag, 1966). We swagger disdainfully past "those sociologists and economists down the hall," boast of our derring-do in overcoming the hardships of the field, and scoff at those who "stay (home) and mess with numbers." We may not die with our boots on, but we could. And we are not shy about saying so (Hackenberg, 1988, p. 184).

But there is more to it than that. *"No understanding of a world is valid without representation of those members' voices"* (Agar, 1996, p. 27, emphasis in original). If ethnographers hope to achieve such understanding and represent it faithfully, then they must interact with those whose lives they wish to study and describe. The more, the better. Besides, lone rangers have little choice; they must get to know their hosts, they must make new friends, and they must depend on these new friends and acquaintances not only for their research needs but also for their social ones. They have no one else, at least not so long as they stay in the field. But when ethnographers are part of a team, they have others more or less like themselves to live and work with and to depend on. They may use their teammates to hide from their hosts, especially in the early days of fieldwork. But even once they settle in, the other members of the team still act as a buffer against the outside, and often very strange, world of the field.

Ethnographers engaged in team research must sacrifice some of the immersion in another cultural system we value so highly, or so it would seem. But in so doing, are other benefits to be gained? We believe so, for team ethnography also has logistical, methodological, and professional values—and they are significant.

What lone ethnographers give up in the "culture shock . . . [that] comes from the sudden immersion in the lifeways of a group different from yourself" (Agar, 1996, p. 100), they gain in a lessening of the loneliness that can overwhelm ethnographers at times and the anxiety, depression, personality disintegration, and self-doubt that may accompany it (Wengle, 1988). Team ethnography offers more than a friendly shoulder or two to cry on. It offers ethnographers the opportunity to consider, if not incorporate, alternative views of their hosts and the lives they lead; in fact, it forces them to do so. Whether these alternative views are presented formally in project seminars, debriefing sessions, and reports, or whether they just pop up in conversations around the coffee pot or over a beer, they expand the experiences of each team member *and* challenge their interpretations of what is going on.

> If several people examine a similar area, the differences in their biases will generate contradictions in their reports. Contradictions, rather than being viewed as threatening, should be seen as the beginning of a better question, a signpost pointing to a more sensitive understanding. Too many potentially rich contradictions get lost in the politeness of academic rhetoric. (Agar, 1996, p. 99)

* * *

Sunday night I got a call from Tom's [Tavern] saying that Stewart was back in town and to come on down. About 9:30 I walked down, leaving the car with Mark. Joyce, Stewart, and John (a local black who sells vacuum cleaners and likes to hit on white women) played darts, and then when Mark came down, we started a Trivial Pursuit game.

We were in the back room at a table underneath the TV. As often happens, all of a sudden Joyce goes racing over . . . to the area of the pool table. She separated an Anglo woman and a Hispanic man and took the man outside and stood outside with him, talking in what appeared to be a rather amicable manner. I wandered up to the bar to see what was up. The woman—in her mid-30s—was standing at the bar by the pool table, red with rage. She was screaming at the guy who had left, "You fucking Mexican, you better not do anything to my car." Then she would say to the white guy next to her, "It's my table." People said that the reason she had gotten so angry was that the Hispanic had erased her name from the chalkboard that determines the order of play on the table. It must be understood that most of the people in the bar at that time were Hispanic; there was one American Indian and one black.

After she quit yelling at the guy, a young Hispanic male walked by and said something softly to her—I think it was "chill out"—as he headed to the bathroom. She chased him and pushed him in the back, called him "goddam

Mexican" and not to tell her what to do. He reacted calmly and went in the bathroom. I was surprised at how calmly everyone was taking this outburst and that the woman was not thrown out. Most of the minority folks were talking quietly and kind of laughing—obviously talking about her. The whites were looking embarrassed, and the guy next to her—not with her—was trying to calm her down.

She racked the table and, as she finished, the guy she had pushed was standing with his back to her, talking with someone in one of the booths. She reached up with her foot and nudged him in the back, he turned, and in a belligerent tone she asked if he was next up to play. He said no, he was not playing, and walked across the room and sat with the Indian.

Things calmed down, or so I thought, and I returned to Stewart. Mark had left in the meantime, and I asked Stewart to give me a ride home. We left a little after midnight.

Monday night I interviewed Joyce and we talked further about the incident (see tape). She said that the guy [who the woman] was yelling at was her live-in boyfriend of 6 years. He had come down to the bar to get her to leave and evidently had erased her name from the board as part of their argument. Joyce said that this was one reason why the other Hispanics had been so cool—they felt it was a domestic issue and his responsibility, not theirs.

She also said that she had again become belligerent after I left, calling people "fucking Mexicans" and other insults. Joyce had finally kicked her out. Finally the Hispanics had enough; when she would insult them, they would hiss at her, and when Joyce kicked her out (the woman slipped and fell going out the door and narrowly missed splitting her head open) they cheered.

The incident led to a rather heated "discussion" between Art and I. I kept him informed of the incident and updated him as I learned more of it. After I told him of the fact that she lived with the guy, I went on to say something about [there being] more to the incident than just racism. He called the woman a bigot and felt that term provided a satisfactory explanation of the incident. I agreed that she was a bigot and a racist but disagreed that was all there was to the incident. I felt that she was using the most powerful weapons at her disposal to get at her boyfriend (in this case racial slurs) but that probably there were other, perhaps more salient, underlying factors at work.

I got back on my soapbox about racism being situational, that people like [those in Tom's] could be incredibly racist in certain areas and at certain times, while at other times, with the same people, be caring, fair-minded people. Art countered by saying that they were bigots and [that] he didn't even like being around them. . . . I said, "Don't go in there, then."

He said that the people in Tom's were the ones who had kept the local Hispanics down economically and socially; I countered by saying that it was not the people in Tom's but those at the country club. I said that many of the people in Tom's were no higher socially than local Hispanics and contrasted

Art, an Anglo [meatpacking worker and regular in Tom's] with Bobby, a Hispanic [line supervisor at Art's plant and regular in Tom's] (he is often referred to as "half Mexican"). He disagreed.

We argued back and forth, me saying it is a complex phenomenon and we need to understand it and [that] merely writing off such behavior as bigotry and such people as nothing more than bigots is too simple and convenient, like using culture to explain behavior—it explains nothing. Art countered by saying that it was an emotional issue and that I was trying to look at it objectively and [that] someone in his situation (a Hispanic who has been subjected to such discrimination all his life) could not. I countered by saying that we were here to look at the community objectively and to try to *understand* what was going on. We then got into how I couldn't understand how it felt; I agreed but countered with how I grew up in a prejudiced community and environment and the baggage that brought along.

This is the same argument I had with Jose, and it disturbs me. . . . We all identify with the people we work with, and Art is identifying with "his people"; I am identifying with "my people" and seeing the world through their eyes, though I hope I'm seeing the larger picture and taking much of their information with a grain of salt. . . . But then, as Art pointed out when I said he wasn't being fair in his assessment of [the people in Tom's], "Fair is an Anglo concept," and I could afford to see things this way since my group was on the top. Bingo. (Donald Stull, fieldnotes, May 6, 1989)

Such ethnographic moments—Agar (1996, p. 31) calls them rich points—reveal much about the groups we study. They also can tell us about our craft. Some, no doubt, will argue that they affirm that "the world is all bias, cant, instability, and power" (Moore, 1994, p. 348). Maybe, maybe not. What it does show—and ethnographers have known this all along—is that we know what we know as a function of who we are and how we learned it. If we can talk through what we think we are beginning to understand with others of similar professional training but different histories, then we should come to a fuller, richer understanding.

But this particular ethnographic moment confirms something else about ethnographers and the worlds we study. Those worlds, and the people who occupy them, are forever changed. Tonto really is dead, that "all-purpose native guide, interpreter, source of introductions, and fountain of information to which all impenetrable (or misunderstood) informant statements could be referred" (Hackenberg, 1993, p. 13). He served us well when "the object of our efforts was . . . a bounded set (group, neighborhood, *barrio*) with persistent members, well-described by Tonto, who was related to most of them" (p. 18). But Tonto has passed on as the communities he once represented have been transformed. We now look out over new "ethno-scapes." As we do,

> there are some brute facts about the world of the twentieth century that any ethnography must confront. Central among these facts is the changing social, territorial, and cultural reproduction of group identity. As groups migrate, regroup in new locations, reconstruct their histories, and reconfigure their ethnic "projects," the *ethno* in ethnography takes on a slippery, nonlocalized quality, to which the descriptive practices of anthropology will have to respond. The landscapes of group identity—the ethnoscapes—around the world are no longer familiar anthropological objects insofar as groups are no longer tightly territorialized, spatially bounded, historically unselfconscious, or culturally homogeneous. (Appadurai, 1991, p. 191)

So, the death of Tonto may well foretell the passing of the Lone Ranger (Hackenberg, 1993, p. 13). It will, if he does not change his ways (Rosaldo, 1993, pp. 30-32).

The scene around the pool table at Tom's, and the argument about what to make of it, holds another lesson—a lesson about the line that divides ethnographers and their hosts. Agar (1996) puts his finger on it: "Not only aren't we sure what the core of ethnograph[y] is; we're no longer sure where the edge lies between ethnographer and other" (p. 23).

> The distinction doesn't make any sense anymore. People don't clump into mutually exclusive worlds. Ethnographers and others swim in the same interconnected global soup. . . . There's no lone ethnographer bumping up against a person as a representative of a single group, with the two working off a starting point of mutual incomprehensibility. The *differences* between them are still there. . . . But are the differences *within* a similar perspective or *across* different ones? (pp. 21-22, emphases in original)

Ethnography is a joint venture; it is collaborative. It always has been, but now ethnographers are increasingly willing to acknowledge the vital role their hosts and local colleagues play not only in generating data but also in interpreting them (Agar, 1996, pp. 15-16). So, if we really think about it, if we are really honest with ourselves about what it is we do, the question for the ethnographer becomes not whether to team or not to team; ethnography is by its very nature a team enterprise. The question becomes, What do we want our ethnographic team to look like? Whose understandings shall we include?

Sounds as though the research gang is traveling through a pretty dangerous philosophical canyon. We've pinned the Lone Ranger down and made him cry "uncle," made him admit he really was a team player all along. Now what?

First, we'd best admit that, like it or not, the ethnography of the future is increasingly apt to be done as part of a research team. Ethnographers who enter the field as members of research teams may do so alongside other ethnographers, as in the Changing Relations Project, or as the representative of one of several disciplines, where they may find themselves cowering amid a pack of hostile number crunchers who snap at their heels and call for their heads.

At the close of *Long-Term Field Research in Social Anthropology*, Foster et al. (1979) pose the following questions for those considering long-term projects. They could easily have substituted "team ethnography" for "long-term research," and we do so here.

> The principal question that must be asked about [team ethnography] . . . is not "Is it personally gratifying?" Rather, one must ask, "Does it produce results not so readily obtained, if at all, from more traditional research? And are these results of such significance and importance as to justify the expenditure of money and professional time?" (p. 323)

So, what should the Lone Ethnographer look for when he is ready to ride a new range. Should he partner up? That depends on who he's after and what he's after them for. He may not need a posse to round up those dogies. But if he does, if the range is too wide or too full of multiethnic mavericks, then why not ask some of his partners to join up? Or why not join up with some other bunch of buckaroos? It worked for Roy Rogers and Dale Evans, didn't it?

Teams of ethnographers who have not ridden together before should consciously plan how to share fieldnotes and what those notes will contain. They have to be able to enrich their fieldnote contents with adequate context to make notes useful and comprehensible to team members who were not on the scene and do not have the same background knowledge. Teams also must reach an understanding of who "owns" fieldnotes. Discussions must entail the kinds of fieldnotes to be taken, and common understandings must be reached concerning metanotes about team members' individual work. With an early discussion of metanotes, the team can learn from its emerging relationship with the community; bridge individual gaps in rapport, coverage, or analysis; and develop an organizational microculture that emphasizes the joint, corporate, and relational nature of the ethnographic gazes encompassed within it.

Teams that have worked together also need to warm up, but they are far more likely to recognize the need to share their fieldnotes and record the observations that matter. They have a shared history; they know what to expect of one another, and they have ridden that range before.

In either case, a team compact is a good way to begin. It lays the cards on the table for all to see. Points of concern, whether arising from lack of familiarity with new members of the team or from grudges held against old teammates, can be talked through, worked out, and written up in a compact. If taken seriously at the outset, if put in place at the beginning before fieldwork actually begins, and *if followed* through to the project's conclusion, a compact helps a team avoid many of the problems we have reviewed.

The team compact should be explicit on any and all potential "flash points"; ownership of data and publication policy are two of the most obvious ones. Often overlooked, but important nonetheless, is how long the agreement is to remain in force. This will have a bearing on rights to data and on their use and dissemination.

Teams are made up of players, and players—on athletic teams at least—have roles to play and jobs to do. Roles must be defined, and players must accept and carry them out, no less in the field than on the field. The ethnographer's role is vague, ambiguous, and ever changing, and this can present real opportunities and problems for ethnographic teams. But they must somehow divide up the work and make sure it gets done. Each team member ought to have a niche—certain research tasks and primary rights to certain materials. Each investigator also should have an obligation to collect and maintain part of the project's common data for the benefit of the project at large (Foster et al., 1979, p. 339).

Certain celluloid cowboys and Indians have appeared throughout these pages. One has long been a metaphor for ethnographers and how they do ethnography. Another, guilty by association, often symbolizes who they do it with. We think ethnographers should look to some others who have ridden across the silver and small screens of our youth when they search for heroes—and exemplars for their fieldwork.

Westerns have provided the authors with many of their heroes. Film can provide us with a successful model for team research. Films are made by crews. Each crew member has a clear and complementary role—producer, director, scriptwriter, actors, camera and sound operators, and we mustn't forget the best boy. Some crew members work behind the scenes, some in the limelight; some pull the strings, others go for coffee. But all are necessary if the job is to get done, if the film is to make it to the screen. Team ethnography is not filmmaking, and ethnographers are not western heroes. But both hold lessons for team ethnography—trust, cooperation, responsibility, complementarity.

* * *

Next morning, when at sunrise I started toward the mission to bid them good-bye, a glance at the distant corral showed that they had all gone; and as I strained my eyes to catch a glimpse of them, the last white-topped wagon of the train disappeared over the far-off lava hills whence I had first caught sight of the Valley of Zuni. . . . It was with the most gloomy forebodings that I turned toward the pueblo. . . . I entered my lonely room and sat down in the hammock, burying my face in my hands. I heard no moccasin footstep, but when I roused up again the old governor was standing before me.

"Why is our little brother sad?" he asked.

"Alas!" I replied, "my friends are all gone, and they have left me nothing." (Cushing, 1970, p. 41)

When the Stevensons' white-topped wagons disappeared over the far-off lava hills in that September dawn so long ago, they left Frank Hamilton Cushing to discover ethnography. It is time for ethnographers to rediscover those white-topped wagons before they leave ethnography in the dust once again.

NOTES

1. "And a river went out of Eden to water the garden; and from thence it was parted, and became into four heads" (*Genesis* 2:10).

2. Women have been vital to ethnography since its inception. "Of all the sciences, anthropology has the reputation for being most open to women scholars" (Parezo, 1993a, p. 3). Nevertheless, "anthropology, like other social sciences . . ., was a male-dominated and male-oriented field from its infancy" (p. 5). In recent years, however, women's contributions have been more openly acknowledged (see Parezo, 1993b; Behar & Gordon, 1995). Reflecting the discipline's male bias, ethnographers often are referred to as lone rangers. Perhaps our vernacular should distinguish between annie oakleys and lone rangers, but it does not. Besides, lone rangers need not be men—and ethnographers need not be lone rangers.

3. The third moment—"the reading and reception of an ethnographic text"—is beyond the scope of this work (Van Maanen, 1995a, p. 5). Readers interested in this third moment should consult the larger collection, in which Van Maanen (1995b) presents his triptych of "fieldwork, textwork, and headwork," as well as Clifford and Marcus (1986) and a growing body of postmodernist writings.

63

REFERENCES

Adler, P. A., & Adler, P. (1995). The demography of ethnography. *Journal of Contemporary Ethnography, 24,* 3-29.

Agar, M. H. (1996). *The professional stranger: An informal introduction to ethnography* (2nd ed.). New York: Academic Press.

Alexie, S. (1993). *The Lone Ranger and Tonto fistfight in heaven.* New York: Harper-Collins.

Anderson, B. G. (1990). *First fieldwork: The misadventures of an anthropologist.* Prospect Heights, IL: Waveland.

Appadurai, A. (1991). Global Ethnoscapes: Notes and queries for a transnational anthropology. In R. G. Fox (Ed.), *Recapturing anthropology* (pp. 191-210). Santa Fe, NM: School of American Research Press.

Bach, R. L. (1993). *Changing relations: Newcomers and established residents in U.S. communities—A report to the Ford Foundation by the national board of the Changing Relations Project.* New York: Ford Foundation.

Becker, H. S. (1986). *Writing for social scientists: How to start and finish your thesis, book, or article.* Chicago: University of Chicago Press.

Behar, R., & Gordon, D. A. (1995). *Women writing culture.* Berkeley: University of California Press.

Benson, J. E. (1994). The effects of packinghouse work on Southeast Asian refugee families. In L. Lamphere, A. Stepick, & G. Grenier (Eds.), *Newcomers in the workplace: Immigrants and the restructuring of the U.S. economy* (pp. 99-126). Philadelphia: Temple University Press.

Bernard, H. R. (1994). *Research methods in anthropology: Qualitative and quantitative approaches* (2nd ed.). Thousand Oaks, CA: Sage.

Berreman, G. D. (1962). *Behind many masks: Ethnography and impression management in a Himalayan village* (Monograph 4). Oklahoma City, OK: Society for Applied Anthropology.

Bohannan, P. (1981). Unseen community: The natural history of a research project. In D. A. Messerschmidt (Ed.), *Anthropologists at home in North America: Methods and issues in the study of one's own society* (pp. 29-45). Cambridge, UK: Cambridge University Press.

Broadway, M. J. (1990). Meatpacking and its social and economic consequences for Garden City, Kansas in the 1980s. *Urban Anthropology, 19,* 321-344.

Broadway, M. J. (1991). Nebraska's Economic Development Program (LB775) and its impact upon rural areas. *Great Plains Research, 1,* 324-344.

Clifford, J. (1986). Introduction: Partial truths. In J. Clifford & G. E. Marcus (Eds.), *Writing culture: The poetics and politics of ethnography* (pp. 1-26). Berkeley: University of California Press.

Clifford, J., & Marcus, G. E. (Eds.). (1986). *Writing culture: The poetics and politics of ethnography.* Berkeley: University of California Press.

Cushing, F. H. (1970). *My adventures in Zuni.* Palo Alto, CA: American West. (Originally published in 1882-1883)

Doughty, P. L. (1987). Against the odds: Collaboration and development at Vicos. In D. D. Stull & J. J. Schensul (Eds.), *Collaborative research and social change: Applied anthropology in action* (pp. 129-157). Boulder, CO: Westview.

Douglas, M. (Ed.). (1987). *Constructive drinking: Perspectives on drink from anthropology*. Cambridge, UK: Cambridge University Press.

Downey, G. L., & Rogers, J. D. (1995). On the politics of theorizing in a postmodern academy. *American Anthropologist, 97*, 269-281.

Emerson, R. M., Fretz, R. I., & Shaw, L. L. (1995). *Writing ethnographic fieldnotes*. Chicago: University of Chicago Press.

Erickson, K. C. (1989). Microcomputers and managed anthropological teamwork (MAT). *Practicing Anthropology, 11*(4), 14-15.

Erickson, K. C. (1995). *Skillful butchers in a deskilled packinghouse: An ethnographic study of a boxed-beef plant*. Doctoral dissertation, Department of Anthropology, University of Kansas.

Erickson, K. C. (1996). Muscle power and meat: Rewriting a story of progress. In G. Arvastson & M. Lindqvist (Eds.), *The story of progress* (Studia Ethnologica Upsaliensia 17, pp. 63-75). Uppsala, Sweden: Acta Universitatis Upsaliensis.

Erickson, K. C., Grey, M. A., & Stull, D. D. (1990, May 17). *The causes of certified staff turnover in Garden City, Kansas, public schools*. Final report to Unified School District 457 Turnover Committee, Garden City, KS.

Fine, G. A. (1993). Ten lies of ethnography: Moral dilemmas of field research. *Journal of Contemporary Ethnography, 22*, 267-294.

Firth, R. (1972). From wife to anthropologist. In S. T. Kimball & J. B. Watson (Eds.), *Crossing cultural boundaries: The anthropological experience* (pp. 10-32). San Francisco: Chandler.

Forge, A. (1972). The lonely anthropologist. In S. T. Kimball & J. B. Watson (Eds.), *Crossing cultural boundaries: The anthropological experience* (pp. 292-297). San Francisco: Chandler.

Foster, G. M., Scudder, T., Colson, E., & Kemper, R. V. (1979). Conclusion: The long-term study in perspective. In G. M. Foster, T. Scudder, E. Colson, & R. V. Kemper (Eds.), *Long-term field research in social anthropology* (pp. 323-348). New York: Academic Press.

Fujisaka, S., & Grayzel, J. (1978). Partnership research: A case of divergent ethnographic styles in prison fieldwork. *Human Organization, 37*, 172-179.

Geertz, C. (1988). *Works and lives: The anthropologist as author*. Stanford, CA: Stanford University Press.

Geertz, C. (1995). *After the fact: Two countries, four decades, one anthropologist*. Cambridge, MA: Harvard University Press.

Gibson, M. A. (1987). Collaborative educational ethnography: Problems and profits. In D. D. Stull & J. J. Schensul (Eds.), *Collaborative research for social change: Applied anthropology in action* (pp. 99-125). Boulder, CO: Westview.

Giles, H., & Coupland, N. (1991). *Language: Contexts and consequences*. Northampton, UK: Open University Press.

Golde, P. (1970). *Women in the field: Anthropological experiences*. Chicago: Aldine.

Goode, J. G., & Schneider, J. A. (1994). *Reshaping ethnic and racial relations in Philadelphia: Immigrants in a divided city*. Philadelphia: Temple University Press.

Gouveia, L., & Stull, D. D. (1995). Dances with cows: Beefpacking's impact on Garden City, Kansas, and Lexington, Nebraska. In D. D. Stull, M. J. Broadway, & D. Griffith (Eds.), *Any way you cut it: Meat processing and small-town America* (pp. 85-107). Lawrence: University Press of Kansas.

66

Gow, D. D. (1991). Collaboration in development consulting: Stooges, hired guns, or musketeers. *Human Organization, 50,* 1-15.

Green, J. (Ed.). (1979). *Zuni: Selected writings of Frank Hamilton Cushing.* Lincoln: University of Nebraska Press.

Green, J. (Ed.). (1990). *Cushing at Zuni: The correspondence and journals of Frank Hamilton Cushing, 1879-1884.* Albuquerque: University of New Mexico Press.

Griaul, M. (1957). *Méthode de L'Ethnographie* (Université Faculté des Lettres et Science Humaines, Série "Études et Méthodes," No. 63). Paris: Presses Universitaires de France.

Grogan, M. (1996). *Voices of women aspiring to the superintendency.* Albany: State University of New York Press.

Gronewold, S. (1972). Did Frank Hamilton Cushing go native? In S. T. Kimball & J. B. Watson (Eds.), *Crossing cultural boundaries: The anthropological experience* (pp. 33-50). San Francisco: Chandler.

Hackenberg, R. A. (1988). Scientists or survivors: The future of applied anthropology under maximum uncertainty. In R. T. Trotter (Ed.), *Anthropology tomorrow: Creating practitioner-oriented programs in applied anthropology* (Special Publication No. 24, pp. 170-185). Washington, DC: American Anthropological Association.

Hackenberg, R. A. (1993). Reflections on the death of Tonto and the new ethnographic enterprise. *High Plains Applied Anthropologist, 13,* 12-27.

Hackenberg, R. A. (1994). Deconstructing an applied anthropologist: Unmasking the Lone Ranger. *High Plains Applied Anthropologist, 14,* 115-122.

Haddon, A. C. (1931). Tobacco in New Guinea. *American Anthropologist, 33,* 657-659.

Hill, C. E. (1974). Graduate education in anthropology: Conflicting role identity in fieldwork. *Human Organization, 33,* 408-412.

Hinsley, C. (1983). Ethnographic charisma and scientific routine: Cushing and Fewkes in the American Southwest, 1879-1893. In G. W. Stocking, Jr. (Ed.), *Observers observed: Essays on ethnographic fieldwork* (pp. 53-69). Madison: University of Wisconsin Press.

Hinsley, C. M., & Wilcox, D. R. (1996). *The Southwest in the American imagination: The writings of Sylvester Baxter, 1881-1889.* Tucson: University of Arizona Press.

Horton, J. (1995). *The politics of diversity: Immigration, resistance, and change in Monterey Park, California.* Philadelphia: Temple University Press.

Jackson, J. E. (1990). "I Am a Fieldnote": Fieldnotes as a symbol of professional identity. In R. Sanjek (Ed.), *Fieldnotes: The makings of anthropology* (pp. 3-33). Ithaca, NY: Cornell University Press.

Janesick, V. (1994). The dance of qualitative research design: Metaphor, methodolotry and meaning. In N. K. Denzin & Y. S. Lincoln (Eds.), *The handbook of qualitative research* (pp. 209-219). Thousand Oaks, CA: Sage.

Jessor, R., Graves, T. D., Hanson, R. C., & Jessor, S. L. (1968). *Society, personality, and deviant behavior: A study of a tri-ethnic community.* New York: Holt, Rinehart & Winston.

Johnson, N. B. (1984). Sex, color, and rites of passage in ethnographic research. *Human Organization, 43,* 108-120.

Kim-Gibson, D.-S. (Producer). (1990). *America becoming* [film]. Washington, DC: WETA-TV.

Kleinman, S., & Coop, M. A. (1993). *Emotions and fieldwork* (Qualitative Research Methods series, Vol. 28). Newbury Park, CA: Sage.

Kluckhohn, C. (1944). *Navaho witchcraft.* Boston: Beacon.

Knokke, W. (1994). Gender, ethnicity and technological change. *Economic and Industrial Democracy, 15,* 11-34.

Kuklick, H. (1996). Islands in the Pacific: Biogeography and British anthropology. *American Ethnologist, 23,* 611-638.

Lamphere, L. (1979). The long-term study among the Navajo. In G. M. Foster, T. Scudder, E. Colson, & R. V. Kemper (Eds.), *Long-term field research in social anthropology* (pp. 19-44). New York: Academic Press.

Lamphere, L. (Ed.). (1992). *Structuring diversity: Ethnographic perspectives on the new immigration.* Chicago: University of Chicago Press.

Lamphere, L., Stepick, A., & Grenier, G. (Eds.). (1994). *Newcomers in the workplace: Immigrants and the restructuring of the U.S. economy.* Philadelphia: Temple University Press.

Lee, R. B. (1979). Hunter-gatherers in process: The Kalahari Research Project, 1963-1976. In G. M. Foster, T. Scudder, E. Colson, & R. V. Kemper (Eds.), *Long-term field research in social anthropology* (pp. 303-321). New York: Academic Press.

Lee, R. M. (1995). *Dangerous fieldwork* (Qualitative Research Methods series, Vol. 34). Thousand Oaks, CA: Sage.

Leighton, A. H. (1959). *My name is Legion: Foundations for a theory of man in relation to culture, Vol. 1: The Stirling County study of psychiatric disorder and sociocultural environment.* New York: Basic Books.

Lurie, N. O. (1966). Women in early anthropology. In J. Helm (Ed.), *Pioneers of American anthropology: The early uses of biography* (pp. 29-81). Seattle: University of Washington Press.

Malinowski, B. (1984). *Argonauts of the Western Pacific: An account of native enterprise and adventure in the Archipelagoes of Melanesian New Guinea.* Prospect Heights, IL: Waveland. (Originally published in 1922)

Mead, M. (1970). Field work in the Pacific Islands, 1925-1967. In P. Golde (Ed.), *Women in the field: Anthropological experiences* (pp. 293-331). Chicago: Aldine.

Moore, D. C. (1994). Anthropology is dead, long live anthro(a)pology: Poststructuralism, literary studies, and anthropology's "nervous present." *Journal of Anthropological Research, 50,* 345-365.

Narayan, K. (1993). How native is a "native" anthropologist? *American Anthropologist, 95,* 671-686.

Oliver, S. C. (1974). Ecology and cultural continuity as contributing factors in the social organization of the Plains Indians. In Y. A. Cohen (Ed.), *Man in adaptation: The cultural present* (2nd ed., pp. 302-322). Chicago: Aldine.

Pandey, T. N. (1972). Anthropologists at Zuni. *Proceedings of the American Philosophical Society, 116,* 321-337.

Parezo, N. J. (1993a). Anthropology: The welcoming science. In N. J. Parezo (Ed.), *Hidden scholars: Women anthropologists and the Native American Southwest* (pp. 3-37). Albuquerque: University of New Mexico Press.

Parezo, N. J. (1993b). *Hidden scholars: Women anthropologists and the Native American Southwest.* Albuquerque: University of New Mexico Press.

Parezo, N. J. (1993c). Matilda Coxe Stevenson: Pioneer ethnologist. In N. J. Parezo (Ed.), *Hidden scholars: Women anthropologists and the Native American Southwest* (pp. 38-62). Albuquerque: University of New Mexico Press.

68

Partridge, W. L., & Eddy, E. M. (1987). The development of applied anthropology in America. In E. M. Eddy & W. L. Partridge (Eds.), *Applied anthropology in America* (2nd ed., pp. 3-55). New York: Columbia University Press.

Perlman, M. L. (1970). The comparative method: The single investigator and the team approach. In R. Naroll & R. Cohen (Eds.), *A handbook of method in cultural anthropology* (pp. 353-365). New York: Columbia University Press.

Powell, J. W. (1884). *Third annual report of the Bureau of Ethnology to the secretary of the Smithsonian Institute, 1881-1882.* Washington, DC: Government Printing Office.

Powell, J. W. (1886). *Fourth annual report of the Bureau of Ethnology to the secretary of the Smithsonian Institute, 1882-1883.* Washington, DC: Government Printing Office.

Quiggin, A. H. (1942). *Haddon the head hunter: A short sketch of the life of A. C. Haddon.* Cambridge, UK: Cambridge University Press.

Richardson, L. (1990). *Writing strategies: Reaching diverse audiences* (Sage Qualitative Research Methods series, No. 21). Newbury Park, CA: Sage.

Riesman, D., & Watson, J. (1964). The Sociability Project: A chronicle of frustration and achievement. In P. E. Hammond (Ed.), *Sociologists at work: Essays on the craft of social research* (pp. 235-321). New York: Basic Books.

Rivers, W. H. R. (1906). *The Todas.* London: Macmillan.

Rosaldo, R. (1993). *Culture and truth: The remaking of social analysis.* Boston: Beacon.

Rose, D. (1990). *Living the ethnographic life* (Qualitative Research Methods series, Vol. 23). Newbury Park, CA: Sage.

Sanjek, R. (Ed.). (1990). *Fieldnotes: The makings of anthropology.* Ithaca, NY: Cornell University Press.

Scheper-Hughes, N. (1992). *Death without weeping: The violence of everyday life in Brazil.* Berkeley: University of California Press.

Singh, R., Lele, J., & Martohardjono, G. (1988). Communication in a multilingual society: Some missed opportunities. *Language in Society, 17,* 43-59.

Sontag, S. (1966). The anthropologist as hero. In S. Sontag (Ed.), *Against interpretation* (pp. 69-81). New York: Farrar, Strauss & Giroux.

Spindler, G. D. (Ed.). (1970). *Being an anthropologist: Fieldwork in eleven cultures.* New York: Holt, Rinehart & Winston.

Steward, J. H. (1956). *The people of Puerto Rico: A study in social anthropology.* Urbana: University of Illinois Press.

Stocking, G. W., Jr. (1983). The ethnographer's magic: Fieldwork in British anthropology from Tylor to Malinowski. In G. W. Stocking, Jr. (Ed.), *Observers observed: Essays on ethnographic fieldwork* (pp. 70-120). Madison: University of Wisconsin Press.

Stull, D. D. (1990a). "I Come to the Garden": Changing ethnic relations in Garden City, Kansas. *Urban Anthropology, 19,* 303-320.

Stull, D. D. (Ed.). (1990b). When the packers came to town: Changing ethnic relations in Garden City, Kansas. *Urban Anthropology, 19,* 303-427.

Stull, D. D. (1994). Knock 'em dead: Work on the killfloor of a modern beefpacking plant. In L. Lamphere, A. Stepick, & G. Grenier (Eds.), *Newcomers in the workplace: Immigrants and the restructuring of the U.S. economy* (pp. 44-77). Philadelphia: Temple University Press.

Stull, D. D., Benson, J. E., Broadway, M. J., Campa, A. L., Erickson, K. C., & Grey, M. A. (1990). *Changing relations: Newcomers and established residents in Garden City,*

69

Kansas (final report [No. 172] to the Ford Foundation's Changing Relations Project board). Lawrence: University of Kansas, Institute for Public Policy and Business Research.

Stull, D. D., Broadway, M. J., & Erickson, K. C. (1992). The price of a good steak: Beef packing and its consequences for Garden City, Kansas. In L. Lamphere (Ed.), *Structuring diversity: Ethnographic perspectives on the new immigration* (pp. 35-64). Chicago: University of Chicago Press.

Stull, D. D., Broadway, M. J., & Griffith, D. (Eds.). (1995). *Any way you cut it: Meat processing and small-town America.* Lawrence: University Press of Kansas.

Stull, D. D., Erickson, K., & Giner, M. (1996, April). Management and multi-culturalism: A case study. *Meat & Poultry,* pp. 44-51, 65.

Stull, D. D., & Schensul, J. J. (Eds.). (1987). *Collaborative research and social change: Applied anthropology in action.* Boulder, CO: Westview.

Tedlock, B. (1991). From participant observation to the observation of participation: The emergence of narrative ethnography. *Journal of Anthropological Research, 47,* 69-94.

Tedlock, B. (1995). Works and wives: On the sexual division of textual labor. In R. Behar & D. A. Gordon (Eds.), *Women writing culture* (pp. 267-286). Berkeley: University of California Press.

Thompson, L. (1970). Exploring American Indian communities in depth. In P. Golde (Ed.), *Women in the field: Anthropological experiences* (pp. 45-64). Chicago: Aldine.

Thompson, L., & Joseph, A. (1967). *The Hopi way.* New York: Russell & Russell. (Originally published in 1944)

Tyler, S. A. (1986). Post-modern ethnography: From document of the occult to occult document. In J. Clifford & G. E. Marcus (Eds.), *Writing culture: The poetics and politics of ethnography* (pp. 122-140). Berkeley: University of California Press.

Van Gennep, A. (1960). *The rites of passage.* Chicago: University of Chicago Press.

Van Maanen, J. (1988). *Tales of the field: On writing ethnography.* Chicago: University of Chicago Press.

Van Maanen, J. (1995a). The end of innocence: The ethnography of ethnography. In J. Van Maanen (Ed.), *Representation in ethnography* (pp. 1-35). Thousand Oaks, CA: Sage.

Van Maanen, J. (Ed.). (1995b). *Representation in ethnography.* Thousand Oaks, CA: Sage.

Vogt, E. Z. (1979). The Harvard Chiapas Project: 1957-1975. In G. M. Foster, T. Scudder, E. Colson, & R. V. Kemper (Eds.), *Long-term field research in social anthropology* (pp. 303-321). New York: Academic Press.

Ward, M. C. (1989). *Nest in the wind: Adventures in anthropology on a tropical island.* Prospect Heights, IL: Waveland.

Wax, R. H. (1971). *Doing fieldwork: Warnings and advice.* Chicago: University of Chicago Press.

Wengle, J. L. (1988). *Ethnographers in the field: The psychology of research.* Tuscaloosa: University of Alabama Press.

Wolf, M. (1992). *A thrice-told tale: Feminism, postmodernism, and ethnographic responsibility.* Stanford, CA: Stanford University Press.

Yoggy, G. A. (1996). Prime-time bonanza! The western on television. In R. Aquila (Ed.), *Wanted dead or alive: The American West in popular culture* (pp. 160-187). Urbana: University of Illinois Press.

ABOUT THE AUTHORS

KEN C. ERICKSON is Associate Research Professor in the Department of Sociology at the University of Missouri–Kansas City. He holds a bachelor's degree in anthropology from Washington State University, a master's degree in anthropology from the University of Wyoming, and a doctorate in anthropology from the University of Kansas. For nearly 7 years, he worked as a practicing anthropologist in Kansas state government, designing, managing, and evaluating social service and education programs for Southeast Asian refugees in the Garden City area. Later, he coordinated Bilingual Education and Race, Gender, and National Origin Equity Programs for the Kansas State Department of Education. His publications have appeared in anthropological journals and in edited volumes on U.S. immigrants, immigrants in the workplace, and media anthropology.

DONALD D. STULL is Professor and Chair of Anthropology at the University of Kansas. He received his bachelor's degree in anthropology from the University of Kentucky and his doctorate in cultural anthropology from the University of Colorado, Boulder. He also holds a master's degree in public health from the University of California, Berkeley. He has conducted fieldwork among American Indians in Arizona and Kansas, Mennonites in Kansas and Nebraska, and Kansas state governmental officials. Since 1987, he has studied the meatpacking industry and its consequences for rural communities and workers on the High Plains. He has authored or coauthored some 40 scholarly articles and chapters. In addition, he has produced three nationally distributed documentaries and edited or coedited four collections of original essays including *Collaborative Research and Social Change: Applied Anthropology in Action* (1987) and *Any Way You Cut It: Meat Processing and Small-Town America* (1995).

Qualitative Research Methods

Series Editor
JOHN VAN MAANEN
Massachusetts Institute of Technology

Associate Editors:
Peter K. Manning, *Michigan State University*
& Marc L. Miller, *University of Washington*

Other volumes in this series listed on outside back cover